Prepared in cooperation with the Albuquerque Bernalillo County Water Utility Authority

Water-Level Data for the Albuquerque Basin and Adjacent Areas, Central New Mexico, Period of Record Through September 30, 2008

Open-File Report 2009–1125
Revised July 2010

U.S. Department of the Interior
U.S. Geological Survey

Water-Level Data for the Albuquerque Basin and Adjacent Areas, Central New Mexico, Period of Record Through September 30, 2008

By Joseph E. Beman

Prepared in cooperation with the Albuquerque Bernalillo County Water Utility Authority

Open-File Report 2009–1125

U.S. Department of the Interior
U.S. Geological Survey

U.S. Department of the Interior
KEN SALAZAR, Secretary

U.S. Geological Survey
Suzette M. Kimball, Acting Director

U.S. Geological Survey, Reston, Virginia: 2009
Revised and reprinted: 2010

For more information on the USGS—the Federal source for science about the Earth, its natural and living resources, natural hazards, and the environment, visit http://www.usgs.gov or call 1-888-ASK-USGS

For an overview of USGS information products, including maps, imagery, and publications, visit http://www.usgs.gov/pubprod

To order this and other USGS information products, visit http://store.usgs.gov

Suggested citation:
Beman, J.E., 2008, Water-level data for the Albuquerque Basin and adjacent areas, central New Mexico, period of record through September 30, 2008: U.S. Geological Survey Open-File Report 2009–1125, 37 p.

Contents

Figures

Tables

Conversion Factors and Datum

Multiply	By	To obtain
Length		
foot (ft)	0.3048	meter (m)
mile (mi)	1.609	kilometer (km)
Area		
acre	4,047	square meter (m^2)

Vertical coordinate information is referenced to the National Geodetic Vertical Datum of 1929 (NGVD 29).

Water-Level Data for the Albuquerque Basin and Adjacent Areas, Central New Mexico, Period of Record Through September 30, 2008

By Joseph E. Beman

Abstract

The Albuquerque Basin, located in central New Mexico, is about 100 miles long and 25 to 40 miles wide. The basin is defined as the extent of consolidated and unconsolidated deposits of Tertiary and Quaternary age that encompass the structural Rio Grande Rift within the basin. Drinking-water supplies throughout the basin are currently (2008) obtained solely from ground-water resources. An increase of about 20 percent in the population from 1990 to 2000 also resulted in an increased demand for water. A network of wells was established to monitor changes in ground-water levels throughout the basin from April 1982 through September 1983. This network consisted of 6 wells with analog-to-digital recorders and 27 wells where water levels were measured monthly in 1983. Currently (2008), the network consists of 144 wells and piezometers. This report presents water-level data collected by U.S. Geological Survey personnel at 125 sites through water-year 2008. In addition, data from 19 wells (Sites 127–30, 132–134, 136, 138–142 and 144–149) owned, maintained, and measured by Sandia National Laboratories are presented in this report.

Introduction

The Albuquerque Basin is located in central New Mexico and is about 100 miles long and 25 to 40 miles wide (fig. 1). The basin is defined as the extent of consolidated and unconsolidated deposits of Tertiary and Quaternary age that encompass the structural Rio Grande Rift within the basin (Thorn and others, 1993). The study area extends from about Cochiti Lake south to San Acacia and from Tijeras Canyon west to near the intersection of Interstate 40 and the Bernalillo/Cibola County line. The only perennial stream throughout the length in the basin is the southward-flowing Rio Grande, which approximately bisects the basin.

In 2000, the population of the basin was about 690,000 (Bartolino and Cole, 2002) and the population of Albuquerque (fig. 2) was 448,600 (U.S. Census Bureau, 2001). Whereas the majority of people are concentrated within the Albuquerque city limits, the basin population increased about 20 percent from 1990 to 2000 (Bartolino and Cole, 2002; Thorn and others, 1993). The demand for ground water also has increased because drinking-water supplies throughout the Albuquerque Basin are currently (2008) obtained solely from ground-water resources. In 2009, treated water drawn from the Rio Grande will be incorporated into the city of Albuquerque and Bernalillo County water supplies.

A network of wells was established to monitor changes in ground-water levels throughout the Albuquerque Basin from April 1982 through September 1983. This network consisted of 6 wells with analog-to-digital recorders and 27 wells where water levels were measured monthly. Currently (2008), the network consists of 144 wells and piezometers—66 equipped with continuous recording dataloggers, 59 that are measured by hand semiannually or quarterly, and 19 that are measured by Sandia National Laboratories (SNL) at least once a year.

To better help the Albuquerque Bernalillo County Water Utility Authority (ABCWUA) manage water use, the U.S. Geological Survey (USGS), in cooperation with the ABCWUA, currently (2008) measures and reports water levels from 144 wells and piezometers (table 1). Water-level data collected for the Albuquerque Basin and adjacent areas for the period of record through September 30, 2008, are presented in this report. Monitoring-well locations within the basin and adjacent areas are shown in figure 1; locations within the Albuquerque metropolitan area are shown in figure 2.

Well-Numbering System

The system of numbering wells and piezometers in New Mexico is based on the common subdivision of public lands into sections (fig. 3). The well number, in addition to designating the well, locates the position to the nearest 10-acre tract in the land network. This number (referred to as 'local identifier' in table 1) is divided into four segments. The first segment denotes the township north or south of the New Mexico base line, the second denotes the range east or west of the New Mexico primary meridian, and the third denotes the section. The fourth segment of the number, which consists of three

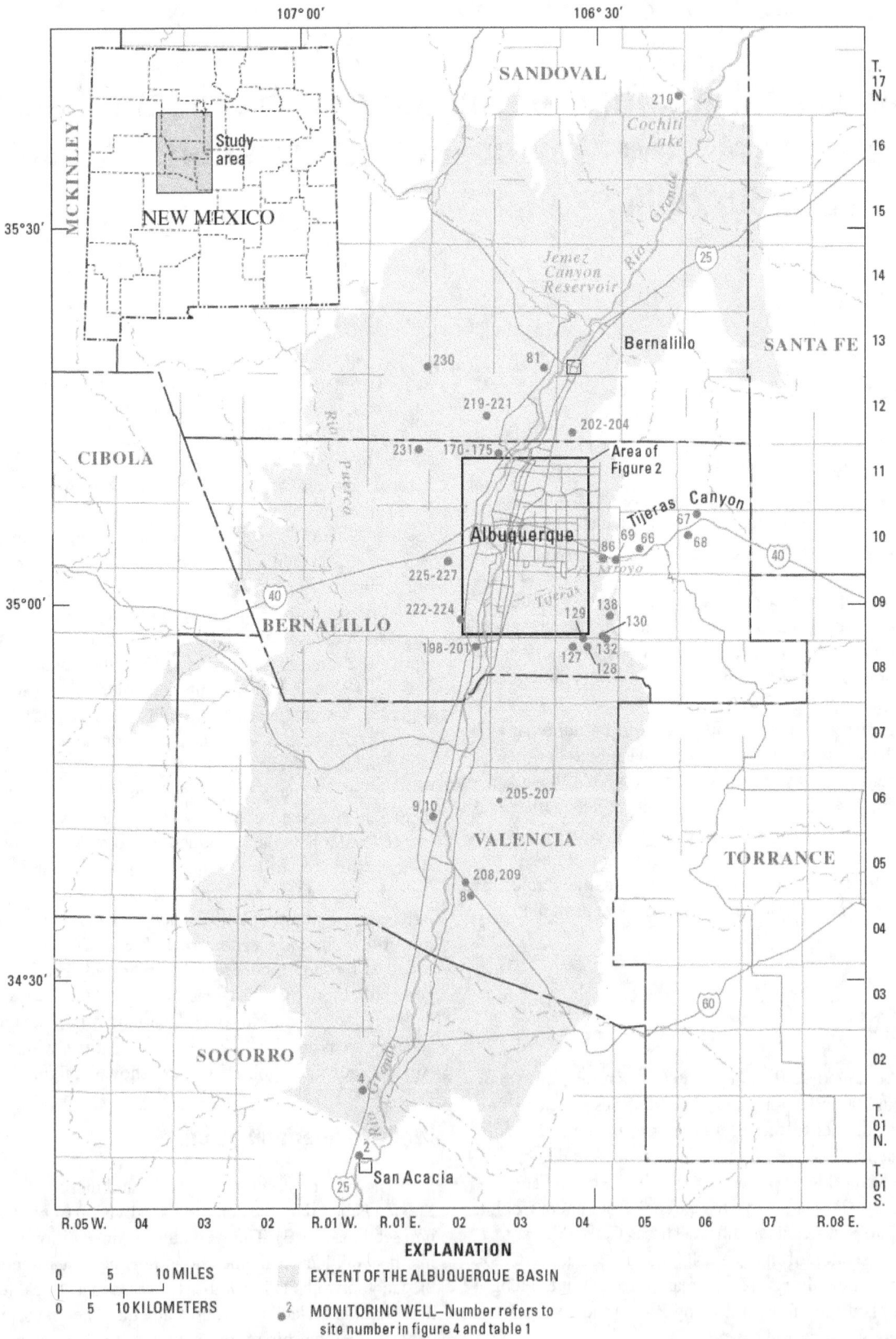

Figure 1.   Location of study area and selected monitoring wells and piezometers in and near the Albuquerque Basin.

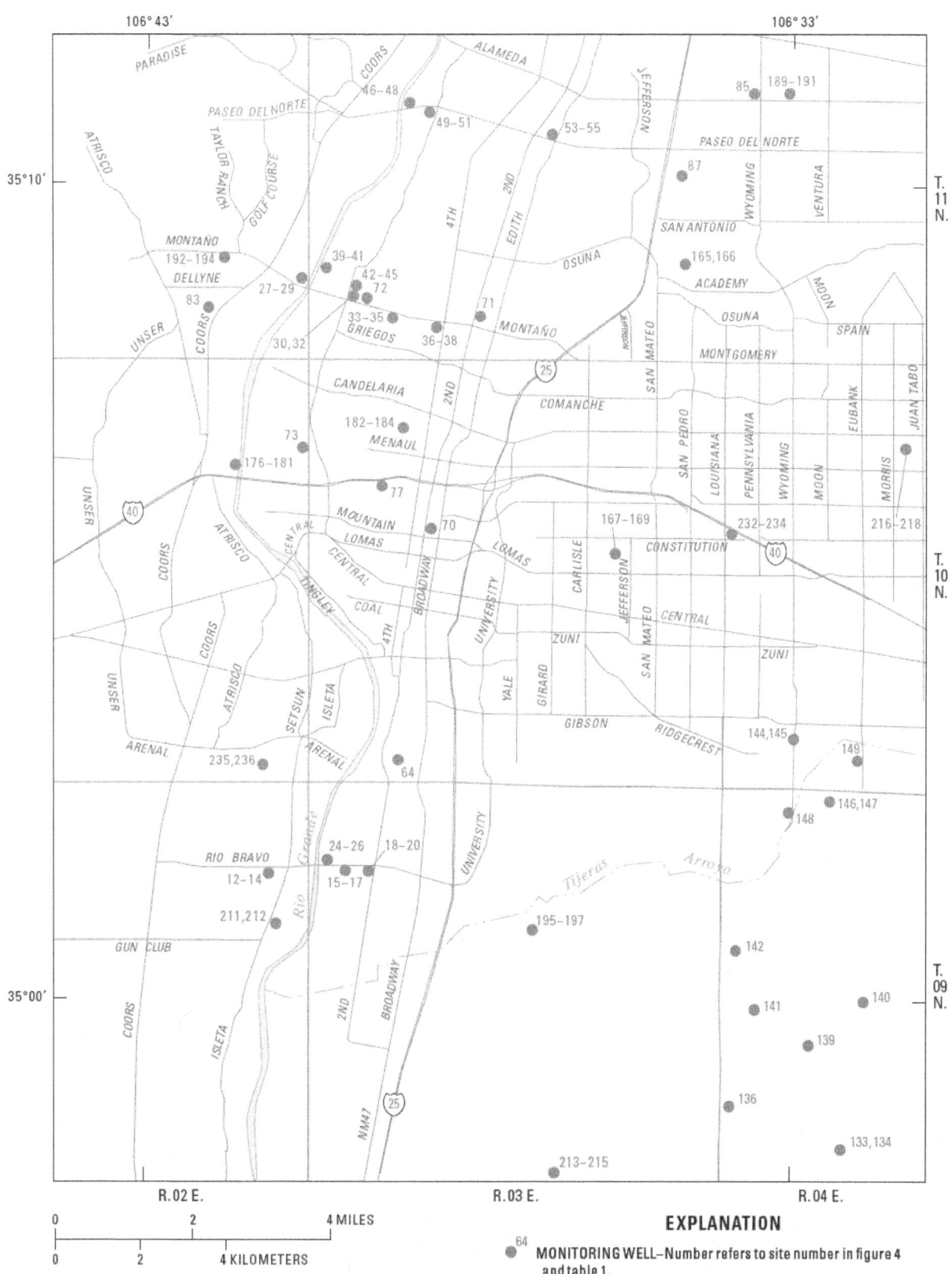

Figure 2.   Location of selected monitoring wells and piezometers within the Albuquerque metropolitan area.

digits, denotes the 160-, 40-, and 10-acre tracts, respectively, in which the well is located. For this purpose, the section is divided into four quarters, numbered 1, 2, 3, and 4, in the normal reading order, for the northwest, northeast, southwest, and southeast quarters. The first digit of the fourth segment gives the quarter section, which is a tract of 160 acres. Similarly, the quarter section is divided into four 40-acre tracts numbered in the same manner, and the second digit denotes the 40-acre tract. Finally, the 40-acre tract is divided into four 10-acre tracts, and the third digit denotes the 10-acre tract. The fourth segment of the well number can further denote subdivisions of the 10-acre tract with more than three digits. Each additional digit further subdivides the tract by quarters in the same manner as shown in figure 3. Letters A, B, C, and so on are added to the last segment of the well number to designate the second, third, fourth, and succeeding wells in the same

tract. For example, well 09N.03E.07.131A is the first well in the NW 1/4 of the SW 1/4 of the NW 1/4 of section 7, T. 09 N., R. 03 E. (fig. 3).

Methods

Electric and steel tapes are used to collect water-level measurements at all 144 wells and piezometers. Pressure transducers and data loggers are used to collect hourly water-level data at sites 42–45 (beginning in November 2005), 165–184, 189–227, and 230–236. Sites 2,4, 8–10, 12–20, 24–51, 53–55, 64, 66–73, 77, 81, 83, and 85–87 are measured semiannually. Sites 230 and 231 are measured quarterly. Sites 127–130, 132–134, 136, 138–142, and 144–149, are measured by SNL personnel with an electric tape at various dates and times throughout the year.

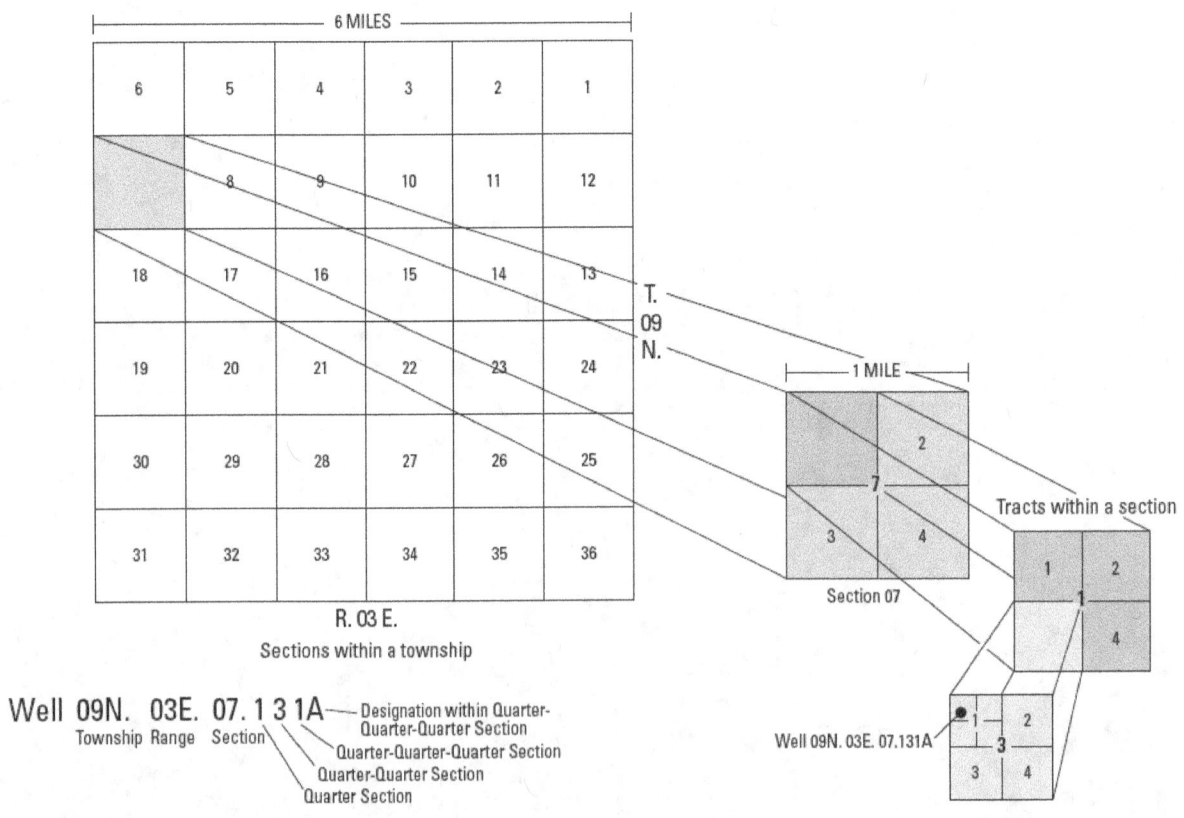

Figure 3.   Well-numbering system in New Mexico.

Table 1. Data from selected wells and piezometers for the Albuquerque Basin, New Mexico.

[--, no data. Discontinuity in numbering sequence is due to wells omitted from this report because of lack of recent data collection. Data from discontinued wells can be seen in previous issues of this report]

Site number	Figure number	Site identifier	Local identifier	Other identifier	Well depth (feet below land surface)	Screened interval (feet below land surface)
2	1	341528106533301	01S.01W.01.213		38	--
4	1	342107106530401	02N.01E.31.313	Sevilleta Refuge Headquarters	223	210–220
8	1	343706106422301	05N.01E.35.143		375	353–373
9	1	344258106460901	06N.02E.30.412A	Estes 1	135	125–130
10	1	344258106460902	06N.02E.30.412B	Estes 5	300	265–270
12	2	350137106410501	09N.02E.12.214A	Rio Bravo Nest 1	148.5	138.5–143.5
13	2	350137106410502	09N.02E.12.214B	Rio Bravo Nest 1	103.8	94–99
14	2	350137106410503	09N.02E.12.214C	Rio Bravo Nest 1	38.4	28–33
15	2	350138106395501	09N.03E.07.131A	Rio Bravo Nest 2	153.5	143.5–148.5
16	2	350138106395502	09N.03E.07.131B	Rio Bravo Nest 2	91.2	81–86
17	2	350138106395503	09N.03E.07.131C	Rio Bravo Nest 2	48.6	38.6–43.6
18	2	350138106393201	09N.03E.07.241A	Rio Bravo Nest 3	148	138–143
19	2	350138106393202	09N.03E.07.241B	Rio Bravo Nest 3	101	91–96
20	2	350138106393203	09N.03E.07.241C	Rio Bravo Nest 3	49.3	39.3–44.3
24	2	350138106401103	09N.03E.07.114B	Rio Bravo Nest 5	515	500–510
25	2	350138106401101	09N.03E.07.114	Rio Bravo Nest 5	150	135–145
26	2	350138106401102	09N.03E.07.114A	Rio Bravo Nest 5	22	7–17
27	2	350854106403701	11N.02E.25.341A	Montaño Nest 1	152	140–145
28	2	350854106403702	11N.02E.25.341B	Montaño Nest 1	93.4	83.4–88.4
29	2	350854106403703	11N.02E.25.341C	Montaño Nest 1	48.4	40–45
30	2	350836106395601	--	Montaño Nest 2	147.4	138–143
32	2	350836106395603	--	Montaño Nest 2	39.7	30–35
33	2	350827106391301	--	Montaño Nest 3	150	140–145
34	2	350827106391302	--	Montaño Nest 3	99	90–95
35	2	350827106391303	--	Montaño Nest 3	50	40–45
36	2	350821106383701	--	Montaño Nest 4	132	123–128
37	2	350821106383702	--	Montaño Nest 4	94	85–90
38	2	350821106383703	--	Montaño Nest 4	50	40–45
39	2	350859106401601	11N.03E.30.313	Montaño Nest 5	25	10–20
40	2	350859106401602	11N.03E.30.313A	Montaño Nest 5	75	60–70
41	2	350859106401603	11N.03E.30.313B	Montaño Nest 5	150	135–145
42	2	350836106395401	11N.03E.31.21311A	Montaño Nest 6	983	972–978
43	2	350836106395402	11N.03E.31.21311B	Montaño Nest 6	836	826–831
44	2	350836106395403	11N.03E.31.21311C	Montaño Nest 6	568	558–563
45	2	350836106395404	11N.03E.31.21311D	Montaño Nest 6	182	172–177
46	2	351059106385903	11N.03E.17.141B	Paseo del Norte Nest 1	600	545–555
47	2	351059106385901	11N.03E.17.141	Paseo del Norte Nest 1	150	135–145
48	2	351059106385902	11N.03E.17.141A	Paseo del Norte Nest 1	25	10–20
49	2	351057106384201	11N.03E.17.233	Paseo del Norte Nest 2	150	135–145
50	2	351057106384202	11N.03E.17.233A	Paseo del Norte Nest 2	95	80–90
51	2	351057106384203	11N.03E.17.233B	Paseo del Norte Nest 2	45	30–40

Table 1. Data from selected wells and piezometers for the Albuquerque Basin, New Mexico.—Continued

[--, no data. Discontinuity in numbering sequence is due to wells omitted from this report because of lack of recent data collection. Data from discontinued wells can be seen in previous issues of this report]

Site number	Figure number	Site identifier	Local identifier	Other identifier	Well depth (feet below land surface)	Screened interval (feet below land surface)
53	2	351035106364703	11N.03E.15.344C	Paseo del Norte Nest 3	544	539–544
54	2	351035106364702	11N.03E.15.344B	Paseo del Norte Nest 3	144	139–144
55	2	351035106364701	11N.03E.15.344A	Paseo del Norte Nest 3	69	64–69
64	2	350256106390801	10N.03E.32.314	San Jose 9	765	188–764
66	1	350359106254701	10N.05E.29.114	Dead Man's Curve	--	--
67	1	350655106194501	10N.06E.05.332	Junction	84	--
68	1	350602106210401	10N.05E.12.434	Home Oil	54	--
69	1	350343106280901	10N.04E.25.324	Granite Hill	--	--
70	2	350548106383901	10N.03E.17.232	City 1	149	139–149
71	2	350824106375301	11N.03E.33.143	City 2	150	140–150
72	2	350837106393801	11N.03E.31.214	City 3	152	142–152
73	2	350646106403601	10N.02E.12.241	City 4	150	140–150
77	2	350618106391801	10N.03E.08.331	BIA Windmill	77	--
81	1	351852106344901	13N.03E.36.132A	San Miguel	206	--
83	2	350829106420401	11N.02E.35.142	La Luz del Sol	250	230–245
85	2	351108106333601	11N.04E.18.124	Spanish Assembly of God	575	--
86	1	350339106294001	10N.04E.26.331	Four Hills	--	--
87	2	351009106344701	11N.03E.24.142	Pino Yard	360	--
127	1	345651106321901	08N.04E.05.413	SFR-1D	378	348–368
128	1	345650106305401	08N.04E.03.313	SFR-4T	377	340–360
129	1	345731106312201	09N.04E.33.414	TRE-1	305	255–295
130	1	345740106292401	09N.04E.35.324	TRN-1	350	320–340
132	1	345732106290502	09N.04E.35.441B	TRS-1D	316.4	266.4–306.4
133	2	345815106321301	09N.04E.32.222A	CWL-MW5L	502	477–497
134	2	345815106321302	09N.04E.32.222B	CWL-MW5U	558	533–553
136	2	345848106335701	09N.04E.30.134	MRN-1	606.7	546.7–586.7
138	1	345919106284001	09N.04E.24.332	School House	103	83–103
139	2	345933106324201	09N.04E.20.321	MWL-MW1	478	456–476
140	2	350001106315701	09N.04E.16.333	AVN-2	520	495–515
141	2	345959106333401	09N.04E.19.211	NWTA-3	460.4	434.9–454.9
142	2	350042106335101	09N.04E.18.142	PL-3	475	445–465
144	2	350225106330301	09N.04E.06.224A	WYO-1	570	510–560
145	2	350225106330302	09N.04E.06.224B	WYO-2	295	265–285
146	2	350232106322801	09N.04E.05.211A	TA2-NW1-325	330.3	295–325
147	2	350232106322802	09N.04E.05.211B	TA2-NW1-595	598	535–555
148	2	350211106315802	09N.04E.04.133	TJA-2	305	275–295
149	2	350318106325701	10N.04E.32.131	PGS-2	--	--
165	2	350908106344401	11N.03E.25.322	Sister Cities	1,308	1,298–1,303
166	2	350908106344402	11N.03E.25.322A	Sister Cities	799	789–794
167	2	350534106354701	10N.03E.14.324	Del Sol Divider	1,567	1,557–1,562
168	2	350534106354702	10N.03E.14.324A	Del Sol Divider	842	832–837

Table 1.   Data from selected wells and piezometers for the Albuquerque Basin, New Mexico.—Continued

[--, no data. Discontinuity in numbering sequence is due to wells omitted from this report because of lack of recent data collection. Data from discontinued wells can be seen in previous issues of this report]

Site number	Figure number	Site identifier	Local identifier	Other identifier	Well depth (feet below land surface)	Screened interval (feet below land surface)
169	2	350534106354703	10N.03E.14.324B	Del Sol Divider	425	315–415
170	1	351201106400501	11N.03E.07.141	Hunters Ridge Nest 1	1,518	1,508–1,513
171	1	351201106400502	11N.03E.07.141A	Hunters Ridge Nest 1	855	845–850
172	1	351201106400503	11N.03E.07.141B	Hunters Ridge Nest 1	238	148–228
173	1	351201106400504	11N.03E.07.141C	Hunters Ridge Nest 2	359	349–354
174	1	351201106400505	11N.03E.07.141D	Hunters Ridge Nest 2	305	295–300
175	1	351201106400506	11N.03E.07.141E	Hunters Ridge Nest 2	263	238–258
176	2	350638106413701	10N.02E.11.244	West Bluff Nest 1	1,095	1,085–1,090
177	2	350638106413702	10N.02E.11.244A	West Bluff Nest 1	689	679–684
178	2	350638106413703	10N.02E.11.244B	West Bluff Nest 1	433	422–427
179	2	350638106413704	10N.02E.11.244C	West Bluff Nest 2	328	318–323
180	2	350638106413705	10N.02E.11.244D	West Bluff Nest 2	254	244–249
181	2	350638106413706	10N.02E.11.244E	West Bluff Nest 2	173	143–163
182	2	350706106390301	10N.03E.05.341	Garfield Park	1,020	995–1,010
183	2	350706106390302	10N.03E.05.341A	Garfield Park	582	552–572
184	2	350706106390303	10N.03E.05.341B	Garfield Park	93	43–83
189	2	351114106330601	11N.04E.18.222	Nor Este	1,525	1,515–1,520
190	2	351114106330602	11N.04E.18.222A	Nor Este	1,193	1,183–1,188
191	2	351114106330603	11N.04E.18.222B	Nor Este	608	538–598
192	2	350910106414801	11N.03E.26.243	Sierra Vista	1,644	1,634–1,639
193	2	350910106414802	11N.03E.26.243A	Sierra Vista	928	918–923
194	2	350910106414803	11N.03E.26.243B	Sierra Vista	205	140–200
195	2	350056106370101	09N.03E.10.334	Montessa Park	1,628	1,618–1,623
196	2	350056106370102	09N.03E.10.334A	Montessa Park	708	698–703
197	2	350056106370103	09N.03E.10.334B	Montessa Park	330	260–320
198	1	345650106415901	08N.02E.02.413	Isleta	1,340	1,330–1,335
199	1	345650106415902	08N.02E.02.413A	Isleta	815	805–810
200	1	345650106415903	08N.02E.02.413B	Isleta	185	175–180
201	1	345650106415904	08N.02E.02.413C	Isleta	50	10–40
202	1	351357106323001	12N.04E.29.433	Sandia Pueblo	1,305	1,295–1,300
203	1	351357106323002	12N.04E.29.433A	Sandia Pueblo	1,025	1,015–1,020
204	1	351357106323003	12N.04E.29.433B	Sandia Pueblo	535	485–525
205	1	344431106393401	06N.03E.18.442	Tomé	1,200	1,185–1,195
206	1	344431106393402	06N.03E.18.442A	Tomé	710	695–705
207	1	344431106393403	06N.03E.18.442B	Tomé	275	225–265
208	1	343753106430601	05N.03E.28.411	Nancy Lopez	1,186	1,166–1,176
209	1	343753106430602	05N.03E.28.411A	Nancy Lopez	695	675–685
210	1	354056106215801	17N.05E.24.344	Dome Road	1,295	1,280–1,290
211	2	350100106405701	09N.02E.12.433	Rio Bravo Park	595	585–590
212	2	350100106405702	09N.02E.12.433A	Rio Bravo Park	210	200–205

Table 1.   Data from selected wells and piezometers for the Albuquerque Basin, New Mexico.—Continued

[--, no data. Discontinuity in numbering sequence is due to wells omitted from this report because of lack of recent data collection. Data from discontinued wells can be seen in previous issues of this report]

Site number	Figure number	Site identifier	Local identifier	Other identifier	Well depth (feet below land surface)	Screened interval (feet below land surface)
213	2	345758106364001	09N.03E.34.231	Mesa del Sol	1,630	1,580–1,620
214	2	345758106364002	09N.03E.34.231A	Mesa del Sol	1,015	990–1,010
215	2	345758106364003	09N.03E.34.231B	Mesa del Sol	525	420–520
216	2	350653106311601	10N.04E.09.214	Matheson Park	1,520	1,460–1,500
217	2	350653106311602	10N.04E.09.214A	Matheson Park	1,045	1,020–1,040
218	2	350653106311603	10N.04E.09.214B	Matheson Park	705	600–700
219	1	351515106410401	12N.02E.24.144	Lincoln Middle School	1,260	1,200–1,240
220	1	351515106410402	12N.02E.24.144A	Lincoln Middle School	835	810–830
221	1	351515106410403	12N.02E.24.144B	Lincoln Middle School	595	490–590
222	1	345842106443101	09N.02E.28.312	Niese Road	1,455	1,445–1,450
223	1	345842106443102	09N.02E.28.312A	Niese Road	960	950–955
224	1	345842106443103	09N.02E.28.312B	Niese Road	297	242–292
225	1	350244106450201	10N.02E.32.433	Westgate Heights Park	1,290	1,280–1,285
226	1	350244106450202	10N.02E.32.433A	Westgate Heights Park	868	858–863
227	1	350244106450203	10N.02E.32.433B	Westgate Heights Park	370	320–360
230	1	352019106474801	13N.01E.24.313	Phoenix Road	1,625	1,600–1,620
231	1	351040106482801	11N.01E.14.342	Paradise Road	1,740	1,720–1,730
232	2	350545106335901	10N.04E.18.133A	Jerry Cline Park	1,462	1,435–1,445
233	2	350545106335902	10N.04E.18.133B	Jerry Cline Park	1,050	1,030–1,040
234	2	350545106335903	10N.04E.18.133C	Jerry Cline Park	510	400–500
235	2	350307106410601	10N.02E.36.321A	Armijo	1,623	1,593–1,613
236	2	350307106410602	10N.02E.36.321B	Armijo	1,025	995–1,015

Well and Piezometer Data and Hydrographs

Data for the 144 wells and piezometers in the network are listed in table 1. Data include site number and identifier, local identifier, other identifier, well depth, and screened interval. Hydrographs of water-level data collected by the USGS are shown in figure 4. The data presented in the hydrographs include depth to water in feet below land surface and hydraulic head, expressed as altitude in feet above the National Geodetic Vertical Datum of 1929 (NGVD 29). Data in graphs from wells that have continuous recorders are shown by lines that represent continuous data. In graphs that present data from periodically measured wells, lines represent time between measurements and are symbolic of water-level trends.

Water-level measurements collected by USGS personnel are presented in 12 previous USGS Open-File Reports (Kues, 1987; Rankin, 1994, 1996, 1998, 1999, 2000; DeWees, 2001, 2002, 2003, 2006; Beman, 2007, 2008).

References Cited

Beman, J.E., 2007, Water-level data for the Albuquerque Basin and adjacent areas, central New Mexico, period of record through September 30, 2006: U.S. Geological Survey Open-File Report 2007–1273, 34 p.

Beman, J.E., 2008, Water-level data for the Albuquerque Basin and adjacent areas, central New Mexico, period of record through September 30, 2007: U.S. Geological Survey Open-File Report 2008–1255, 32 p.

Bartolino, J.R., and Cole, J.C., 2002, Ground-water resources of the Middle Rio Grande Basin, New Mexico: U.S. Geological Survey Circular 1222, 132 p.

DeWees, R.K., 2001, Water-level data for the Albuquerque Basin and adjacent areas, central New Mexico, period of record through 2000: U.S. Geological Survey Open-File Report 01–184, 62 p.

DeWees, R.K., 2002, Water-level data for the Albuquerque Basin and adjacent areas, central New Mexico, period of record through 2001: U.S. Geological Survey Open-File Report 02–312, 41 p.

DeWees, R.K., 2003, Water-level data for the Albuquerque Basin and adjacent areas, central New Mexico, period of record through 2002: U.S. Geological Survey Open-File Report 03–321, 41 p.

DeWees, R.K., 2006, Water-level data for the Albuquerque Basin and adjacent areas, central New Mexico, period of record through 2004: U.S. Geological Survey Open-File Report 2006–1281, 40 p.

Kues, G.E., 1987, Ground-water-level data for the Albuquerque-Belen Basin, New Mexico, through water year 1985: U.S. Geological Survey Open-File Report 87–116, 51 p.

Rankin, D.R., 1994, Water-level data for the Albuquerque Basin, New Mexico, October 1, 1986, through September 30, 1990: U.S. Geological Survey Open-File Report 94–349, 29 p.

Rankin, D.R., 1996, Water-level data for the Albuquerque Basin, New Mexico, period of record through September 30, 1995: U.S. Geological Survey Open-File Report 96–664A, 28 p.

Rankin, D.R., 1998, Water-level data for the Albuquerque Basin, central New Mexico, period of record through 1997: U.S. Geological Survey Open-File Report 98–408, 28 p.

Rankin, D.R., 1999, Water-level data for the Albuquerque Basin and adjacent areas, New Mexico, period of record through 1998: U.S. Geological Survey Open-File Report 99–269, 27 p.

Rankin, D.R., 2000, Water-level data for the Albuquerque Basin and adjacent areas, central New Mexico, period of record through 1999: U.S. Geological Survey Open-File Report 00–231, 62 p.

Thorn, C.R., McAda, D.P., and Kernodle, J.M., 1993, Geohydrologic framework and hydrologic conditions in the Albuquerque Basin, central New Mexico: U.S. Geological Survey Water-Resources Investigations Report 93–4149, 106 p.

U.S. Census Bureau, 2001: State and county quickfacts, accessed July 15, 2002, at *http://quickfacts.census.gov*

Water-Level Data for Selected Wells and Piezometers in the Albuquerque Basin

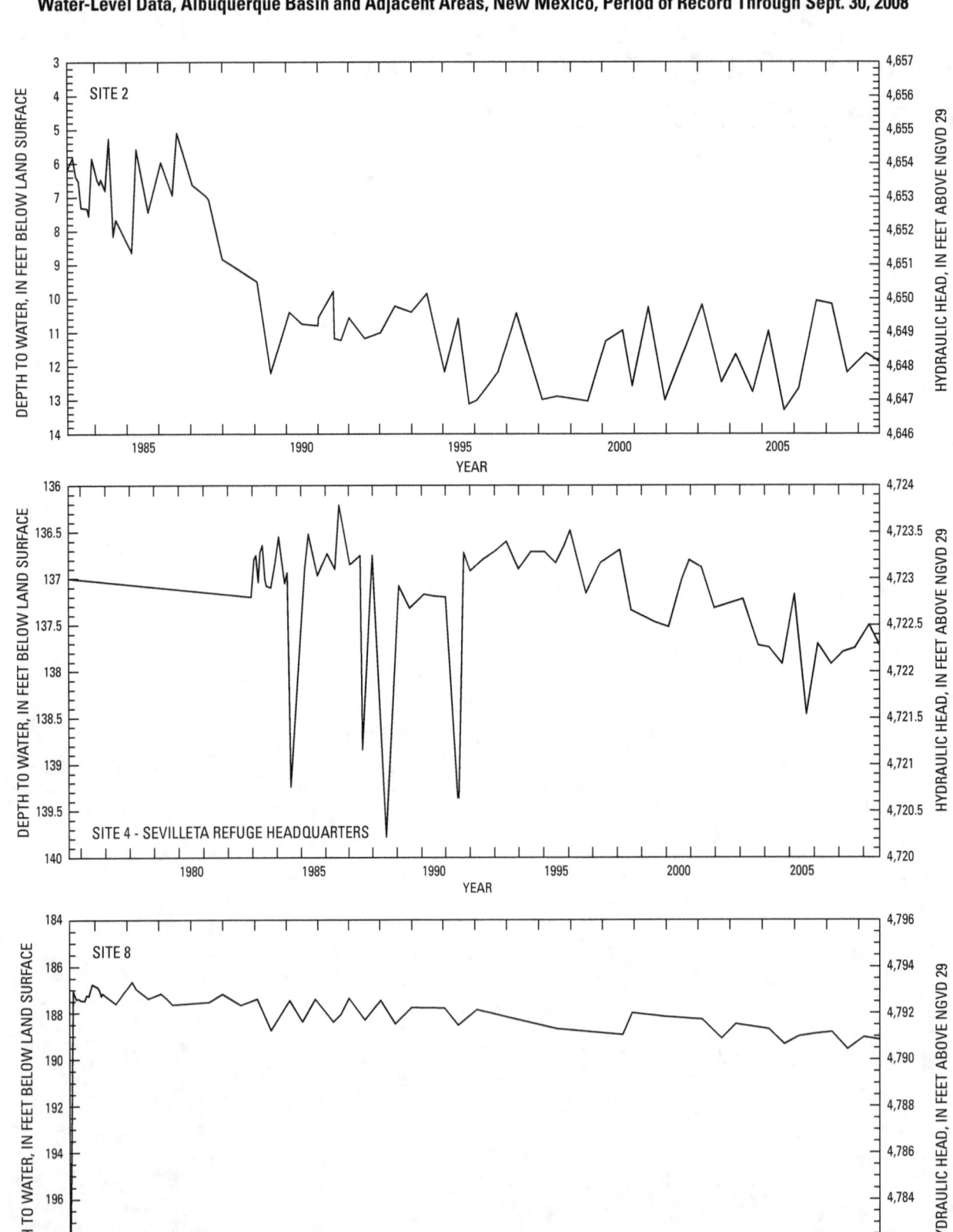

Figure 4.   Water-level data for selected wells and piezometers in the Albuquerque Basin.

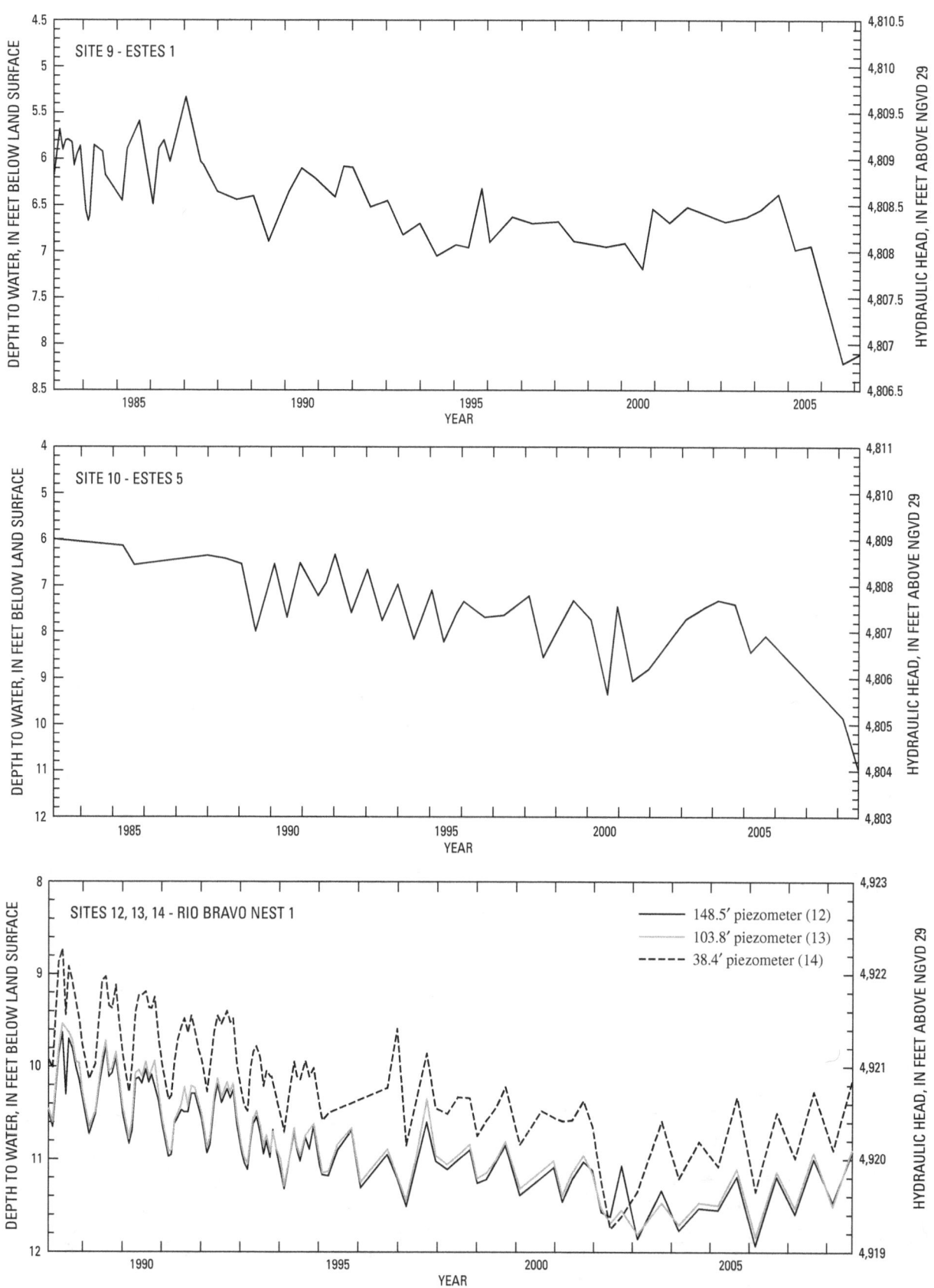

Figure 4. Water-level data for selected wells and piezometers in the Albuquerque Basin.—Continued

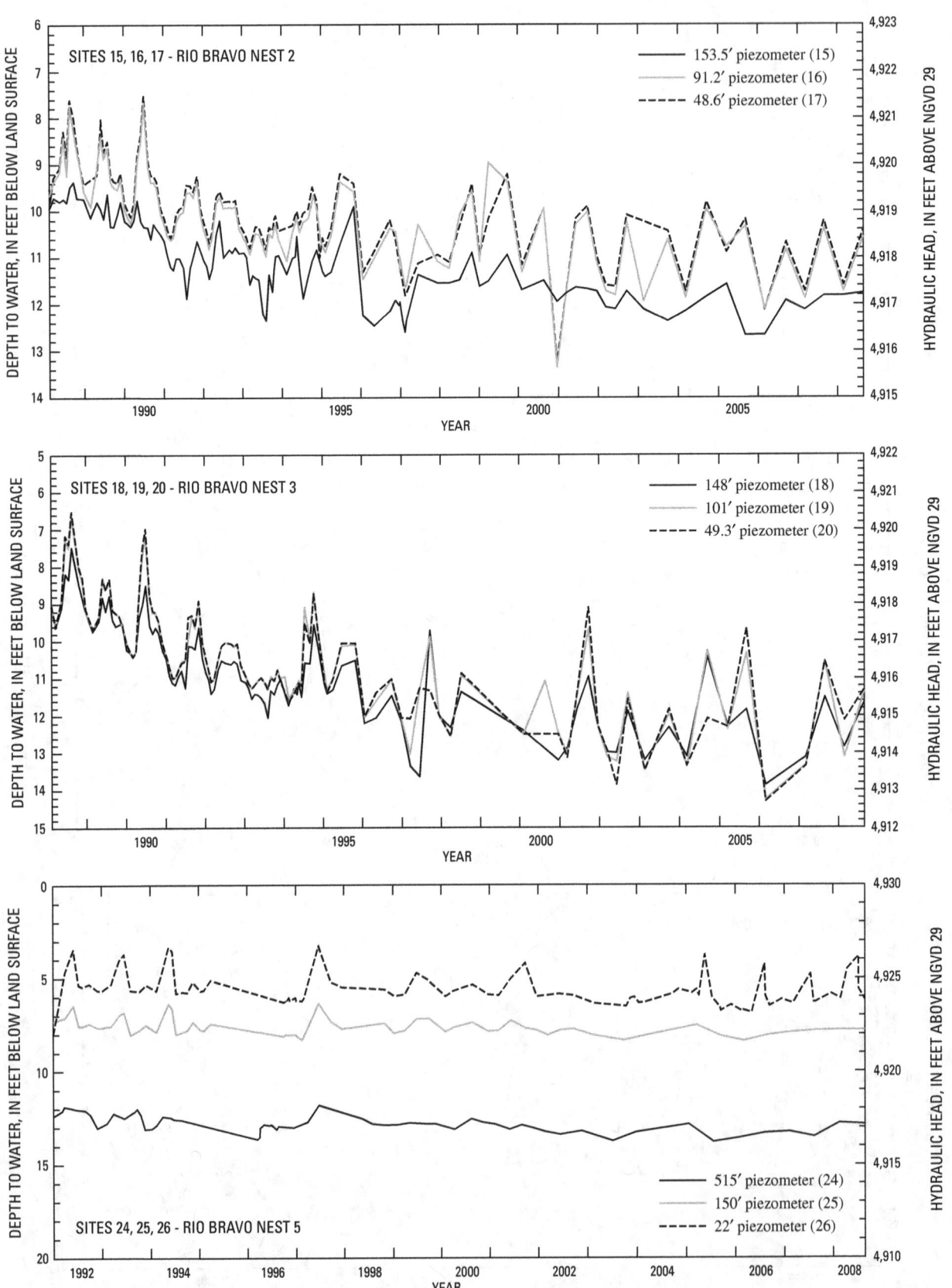

Figure 4. Water-level data for selected wells and piezometers in the Albuquerque Basin.—Continued

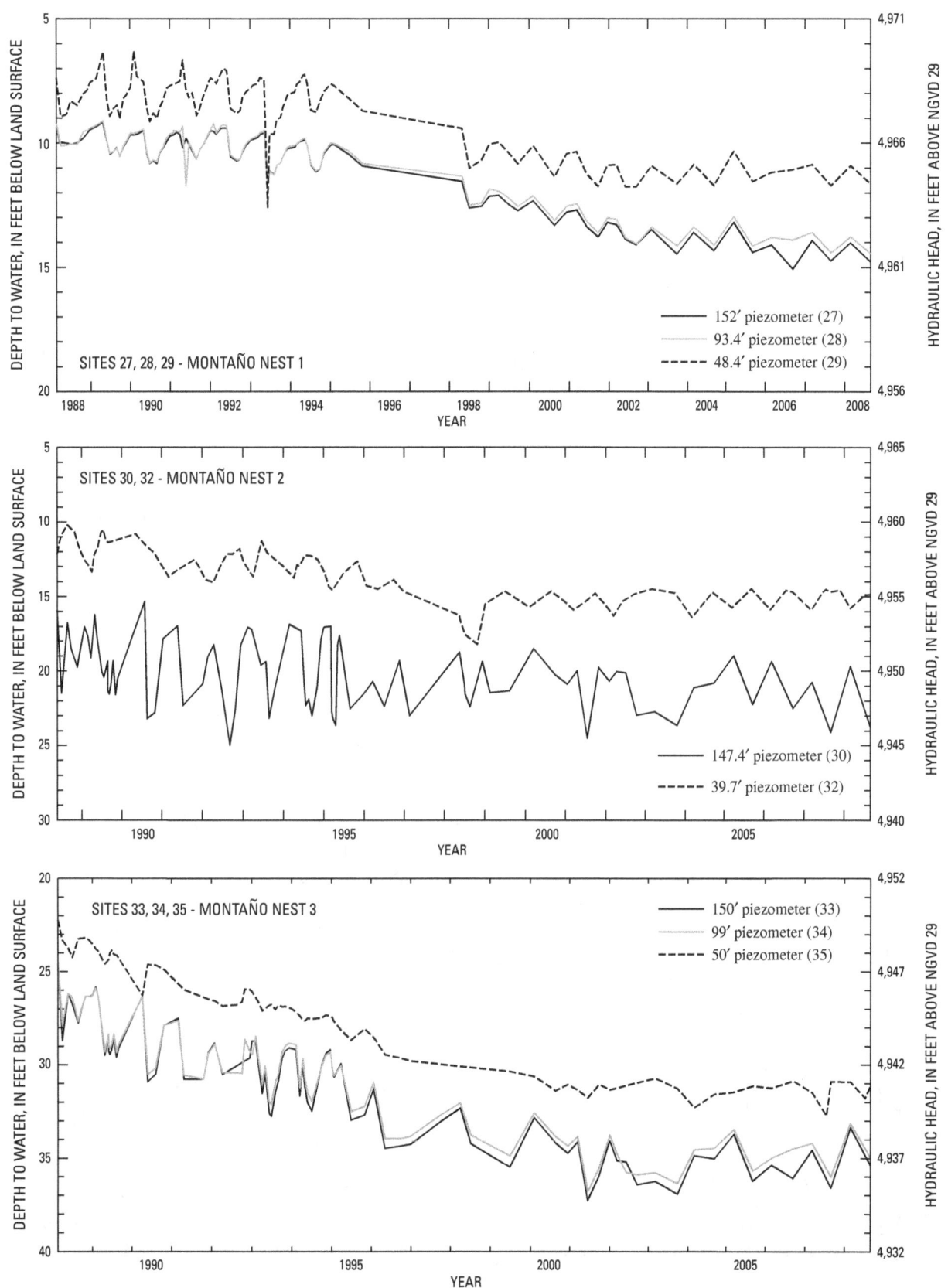

Figure 4. Water-level data for selected wells and piezometers in the Albuquerque Basin.—Continued

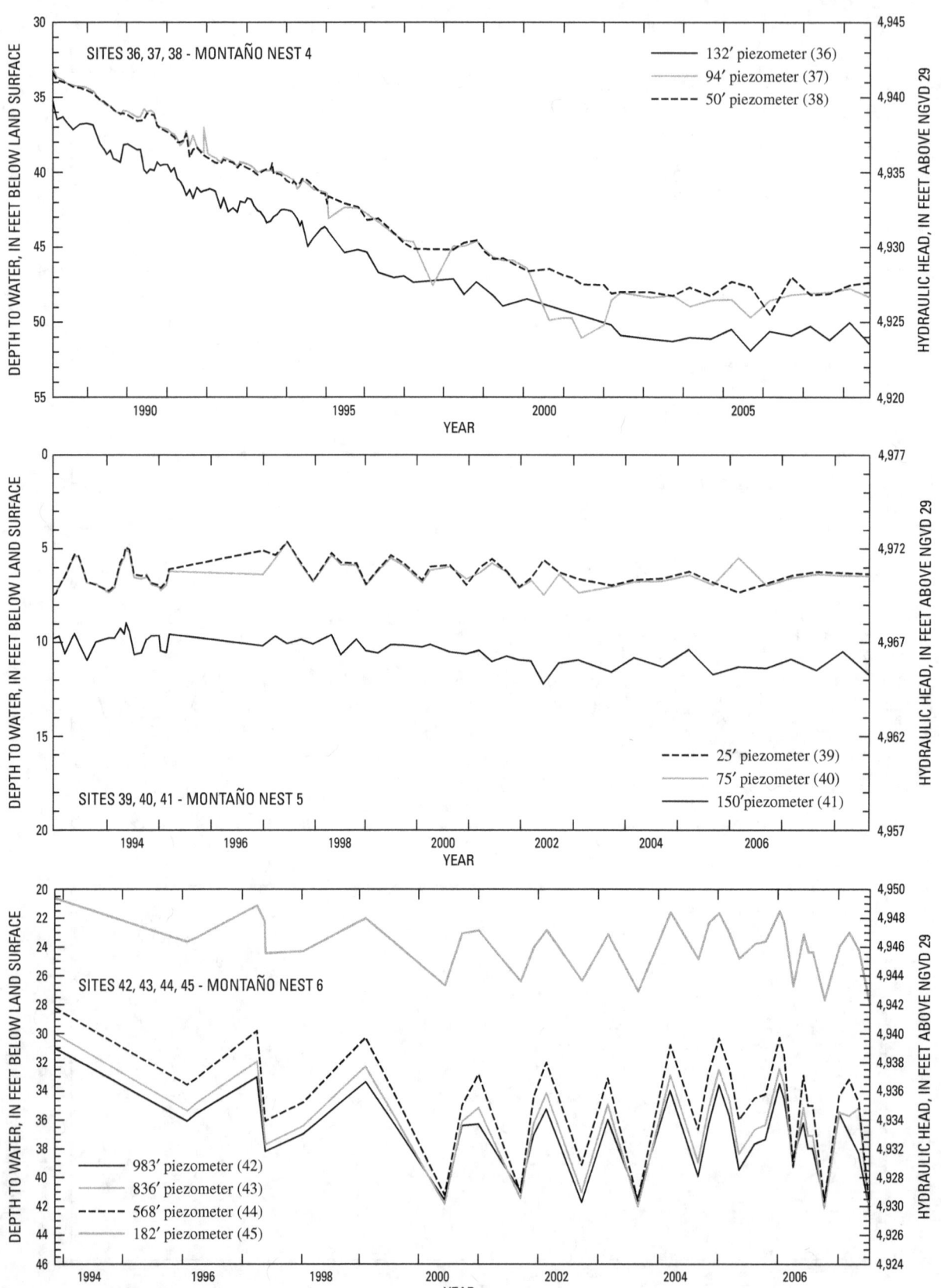

Figure 4.   Water-level data for selected wells and piezometers in the Albuquerque Basin.—Continued

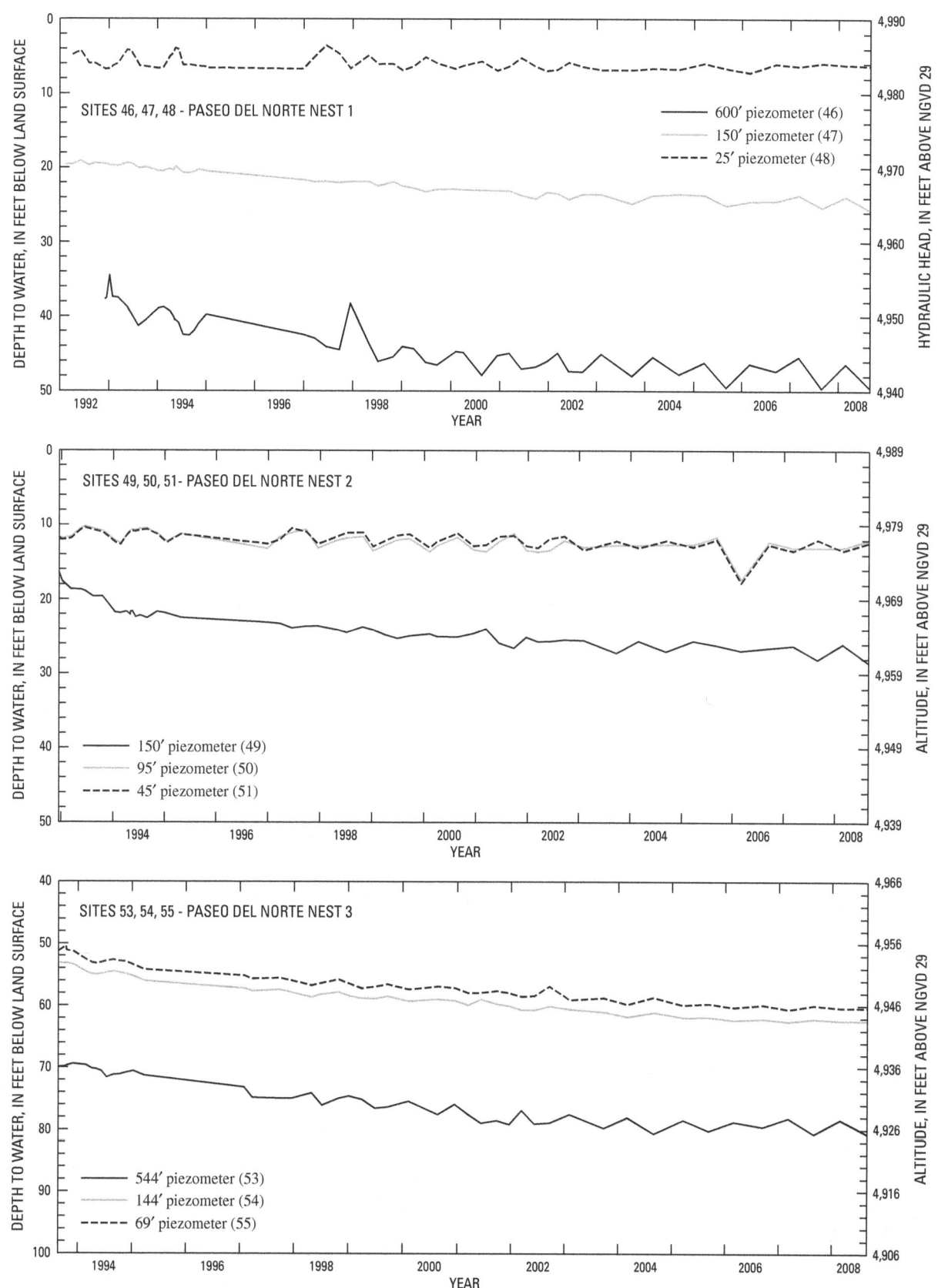

Figure 4. Water-level data for selected wells and piezometers in the Albuquerque Basin.—Continued

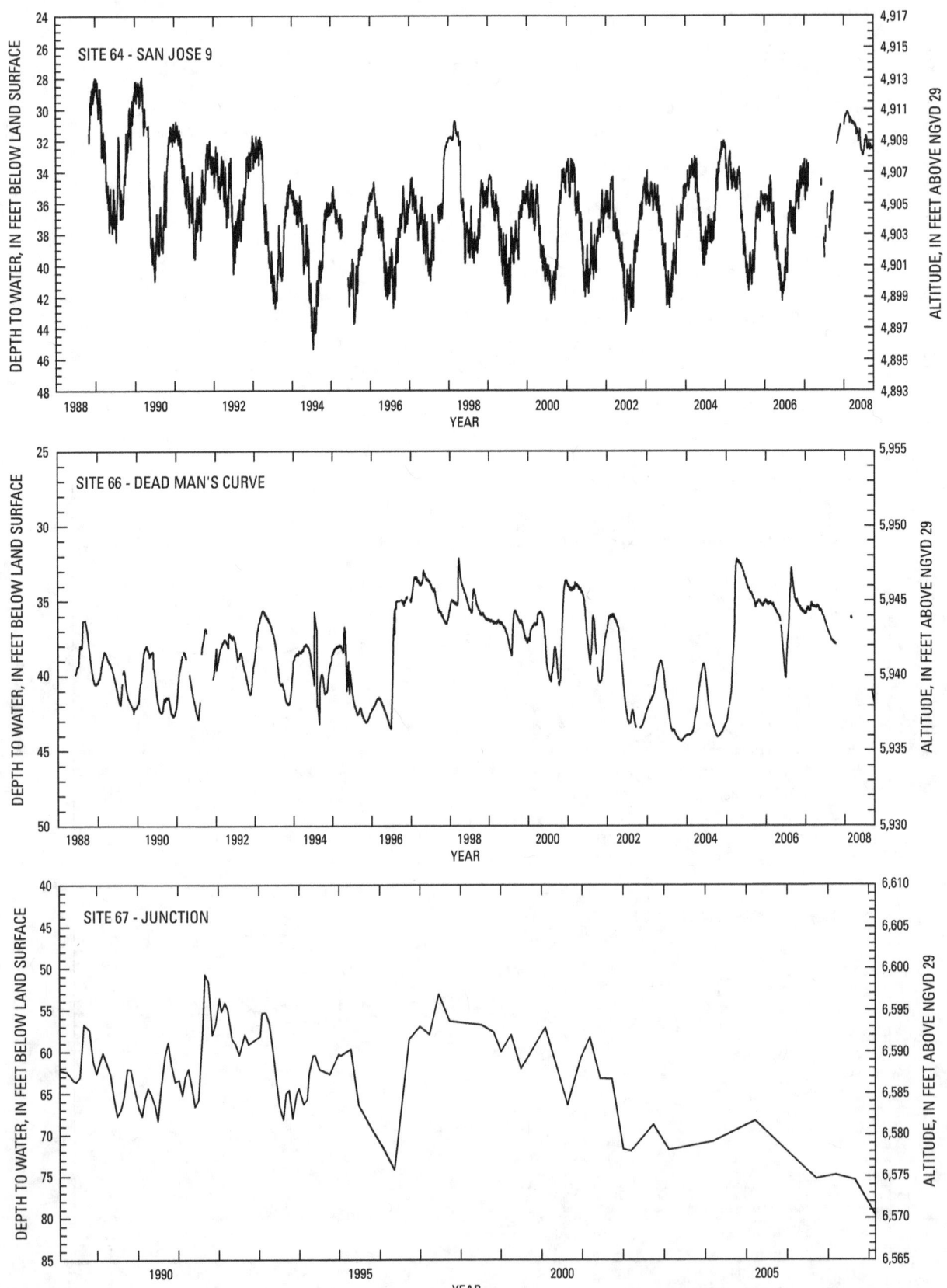

Figure 4. Water-level data for selected wells and piezometers in the Albuquerque Basin.—Continued

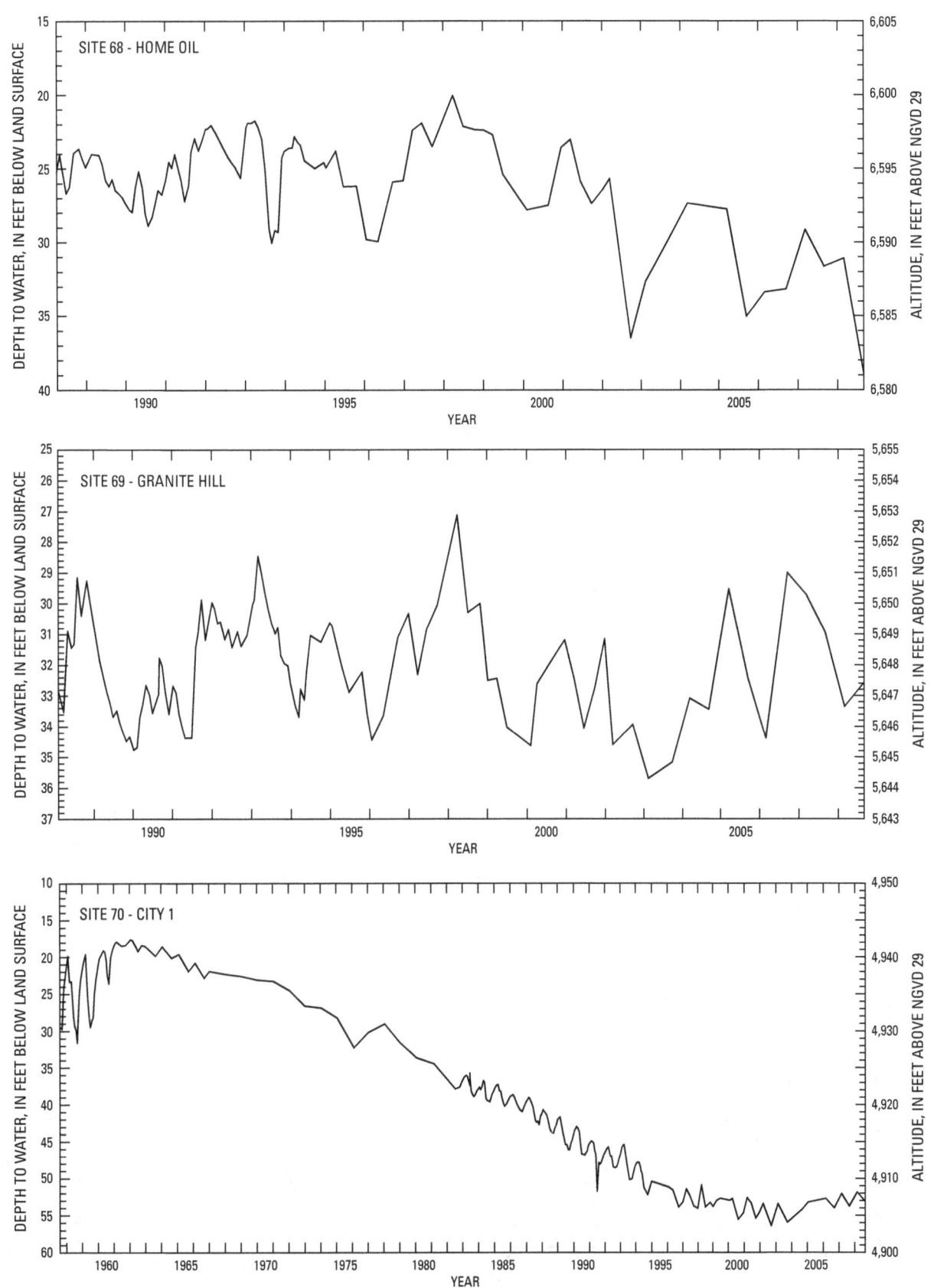

Figure 4. Water-level data for selected wells and piezometers in the Albuquerque Basin.—Continued

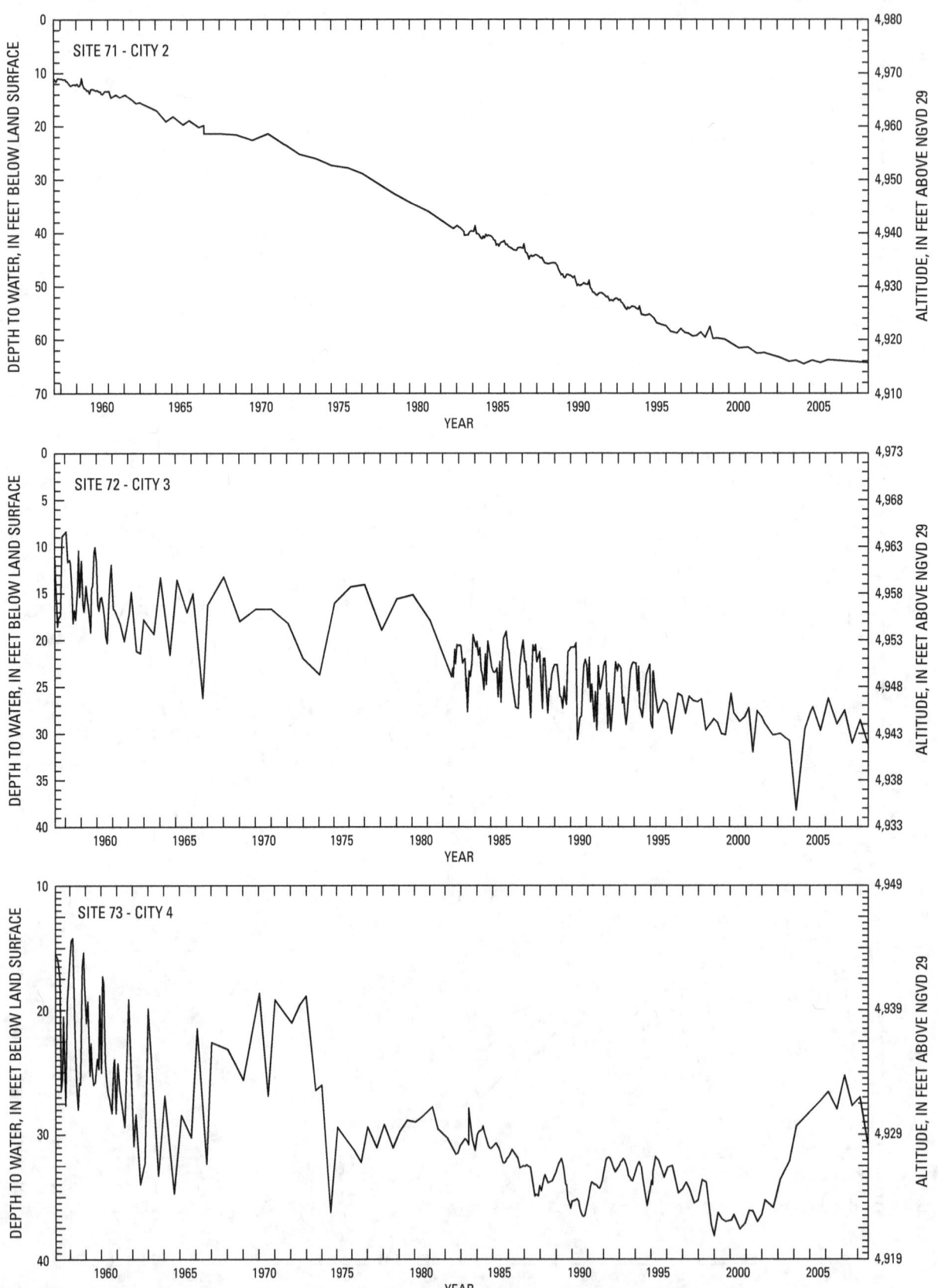

Figure 4.   Water-level data for selected wells and piezometers in the Albuquerque Basin.—Continued

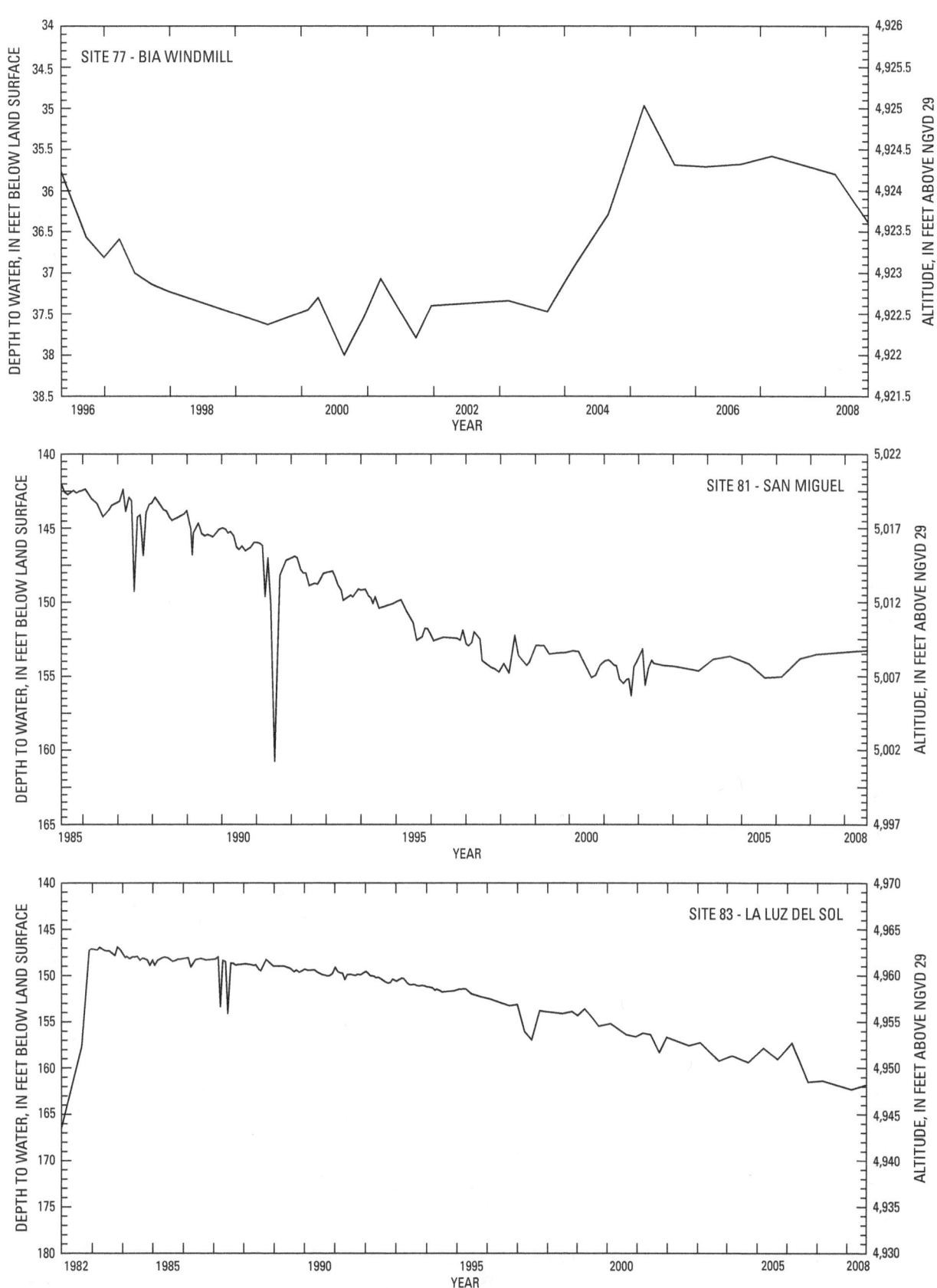

Figure 4.   Water-level data for selected wells and piezometers in the Albuquerque Basin.—Continued

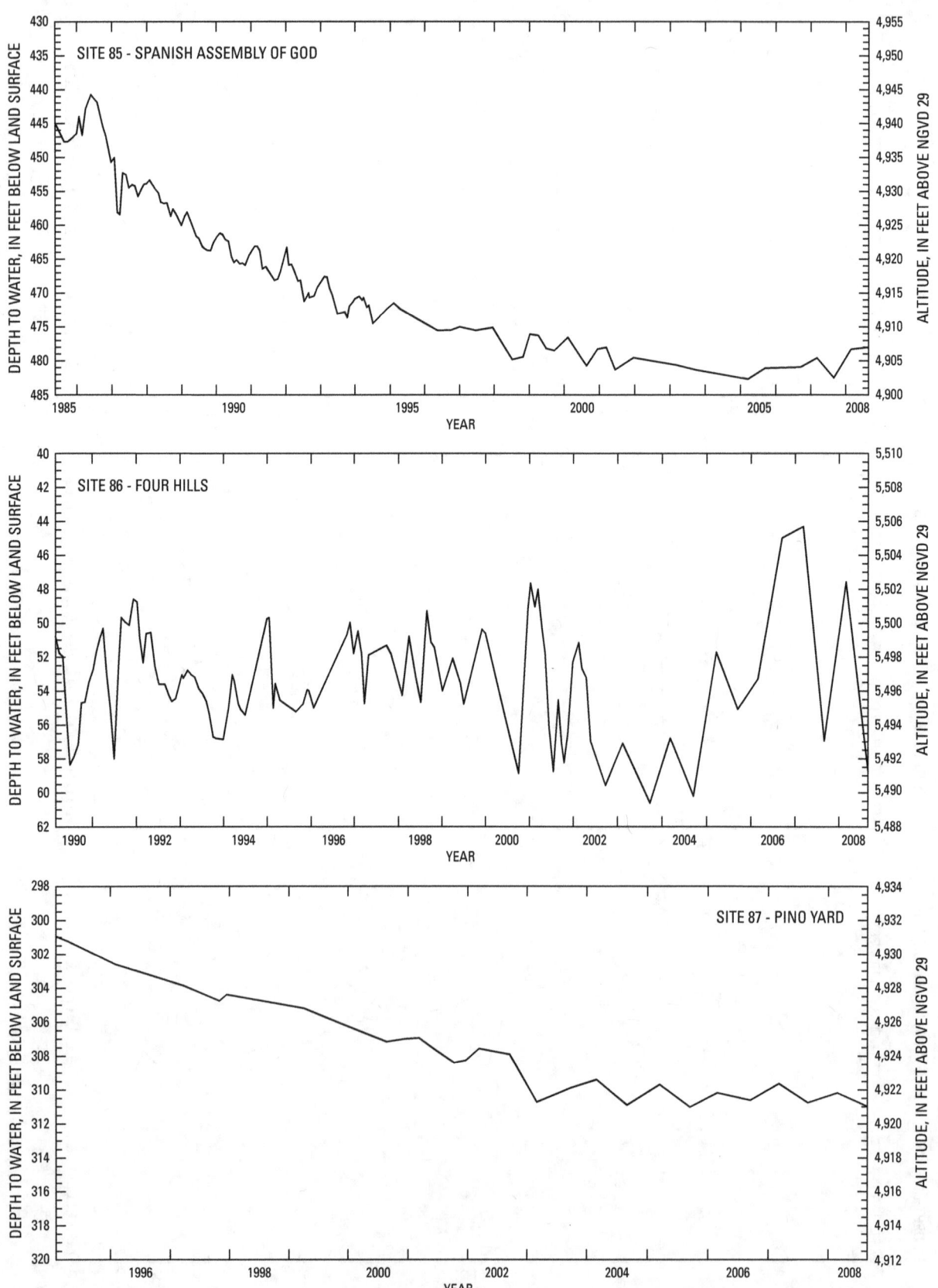

Figure 4.   Water-level data for selected wells and piezometers in the Albuquerque Basin.—Continued

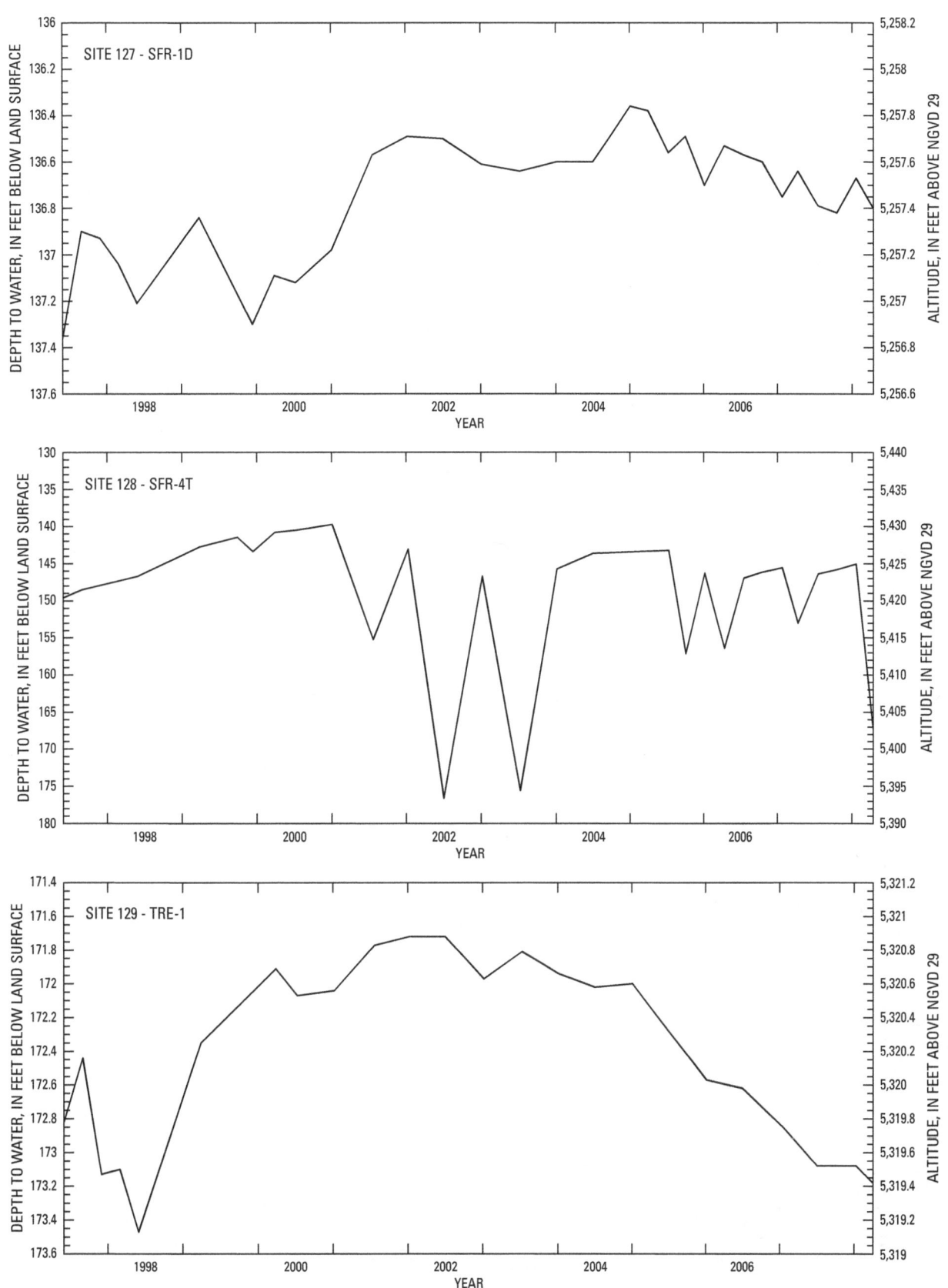

Figure 4. Water-level data for selected wells and piezometers in the Albuquerque Basin.—Continued

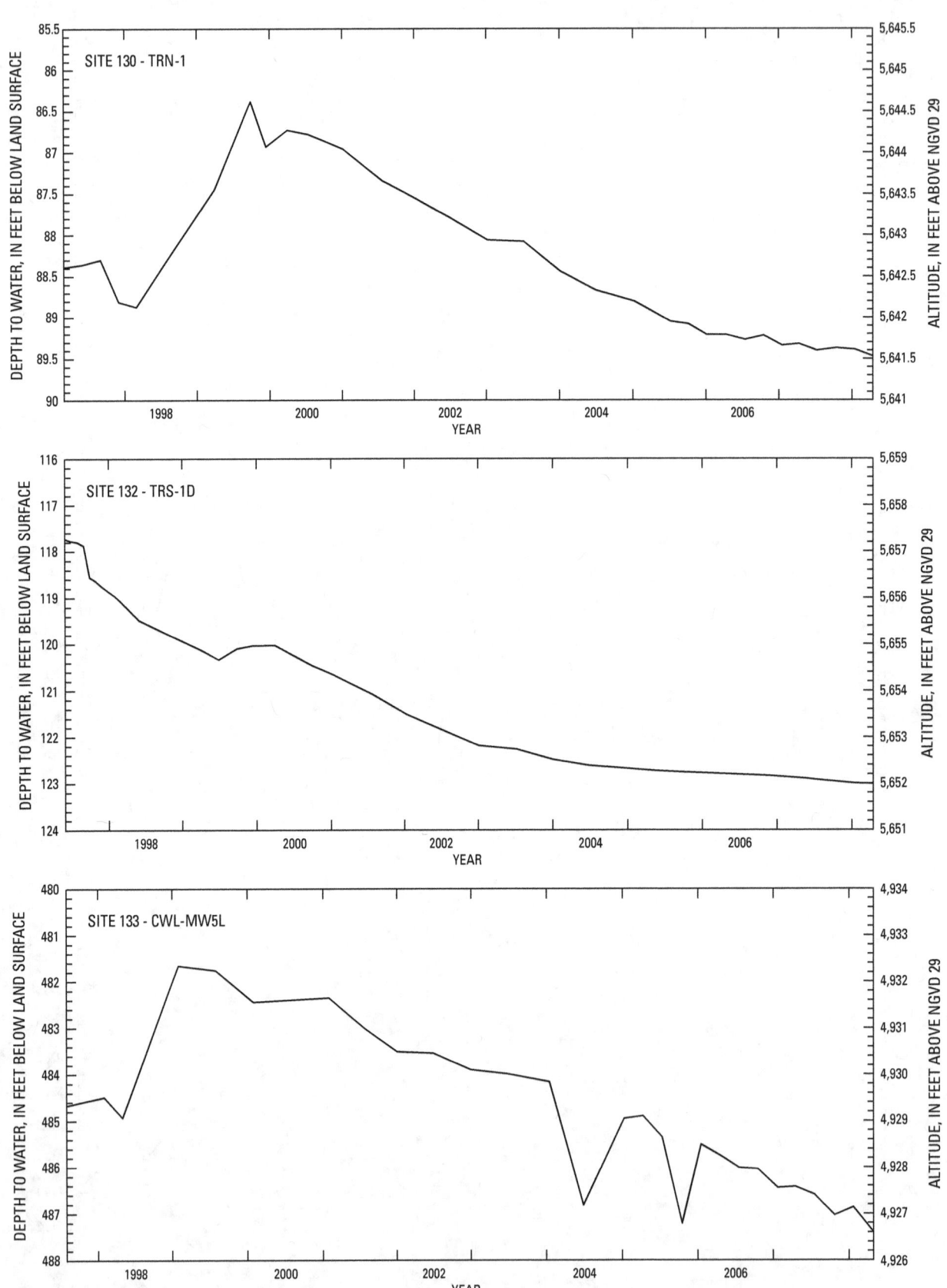

Figure 4.   Water-level data for selected wells and piezometers in the Albuquerque Basin.—Continued

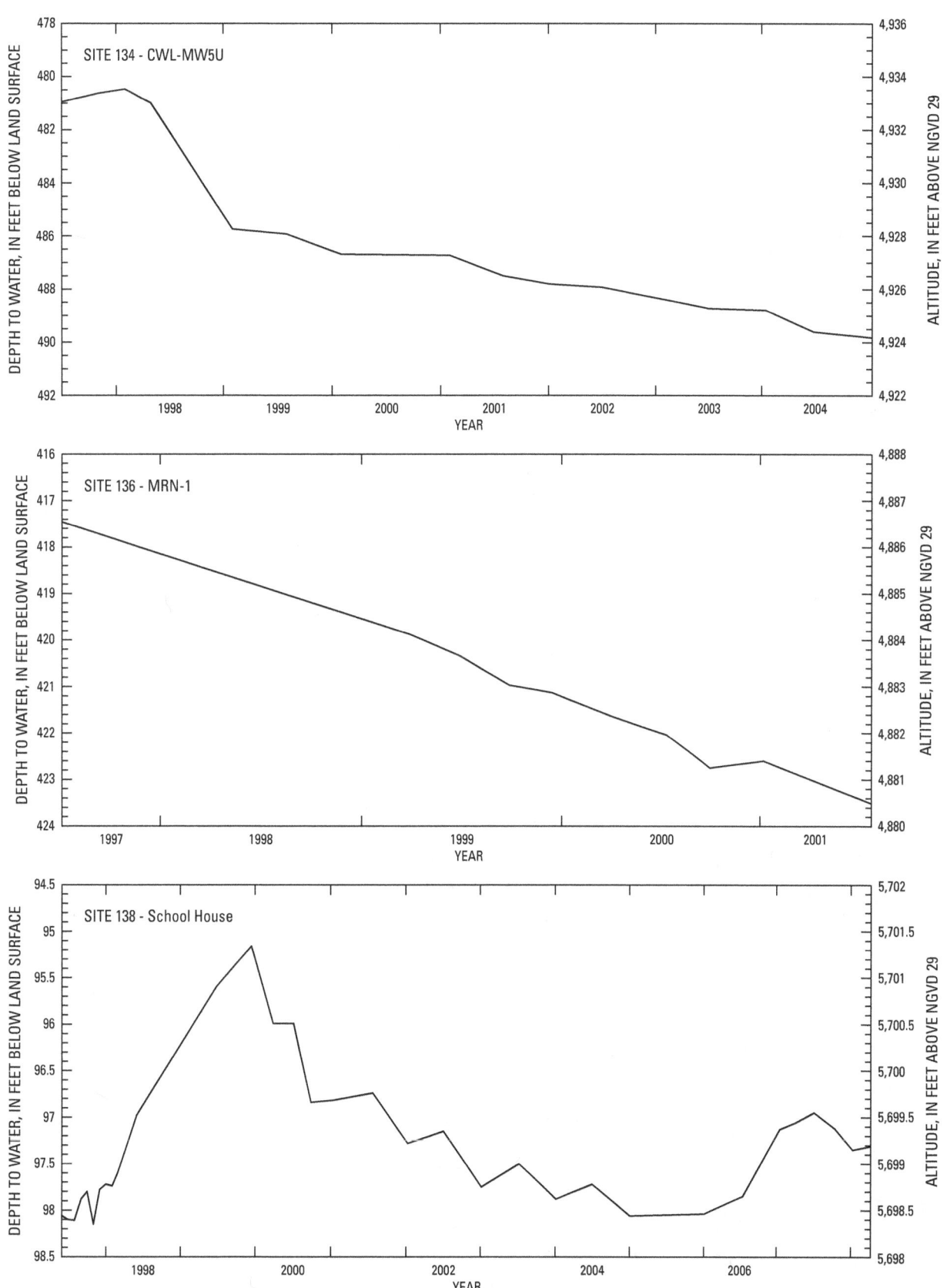

Figure 4. Water-level data for selected wells and piezometers in the Albuquerque Basin.—Continued

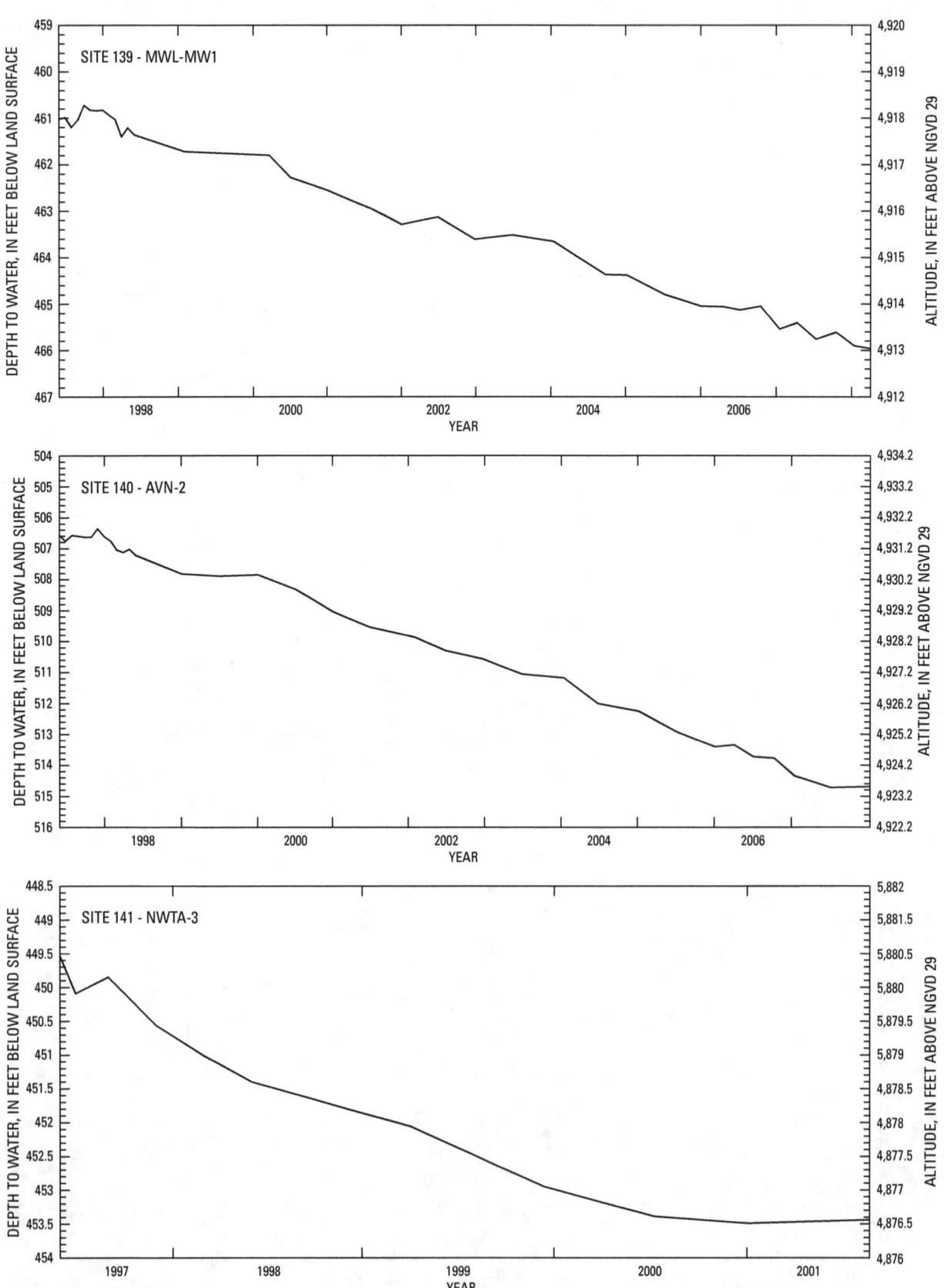

Figure 4. Water-level data for selected wells and piezometers in the Albuquerque Basin.—Continued

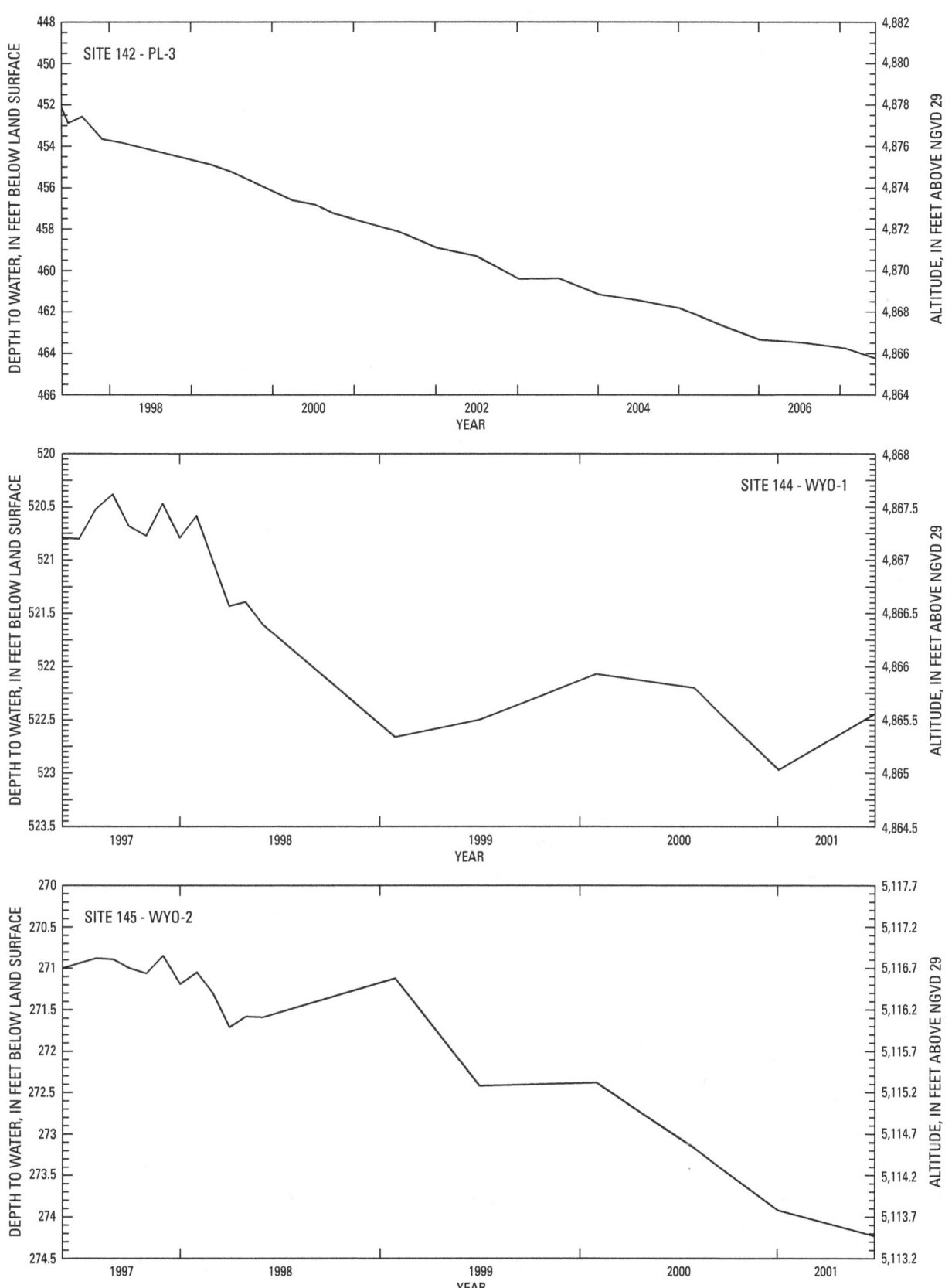

Figure 4. Water-level data for selected wells and piezometers in the Albuquerque Basin.—Continued

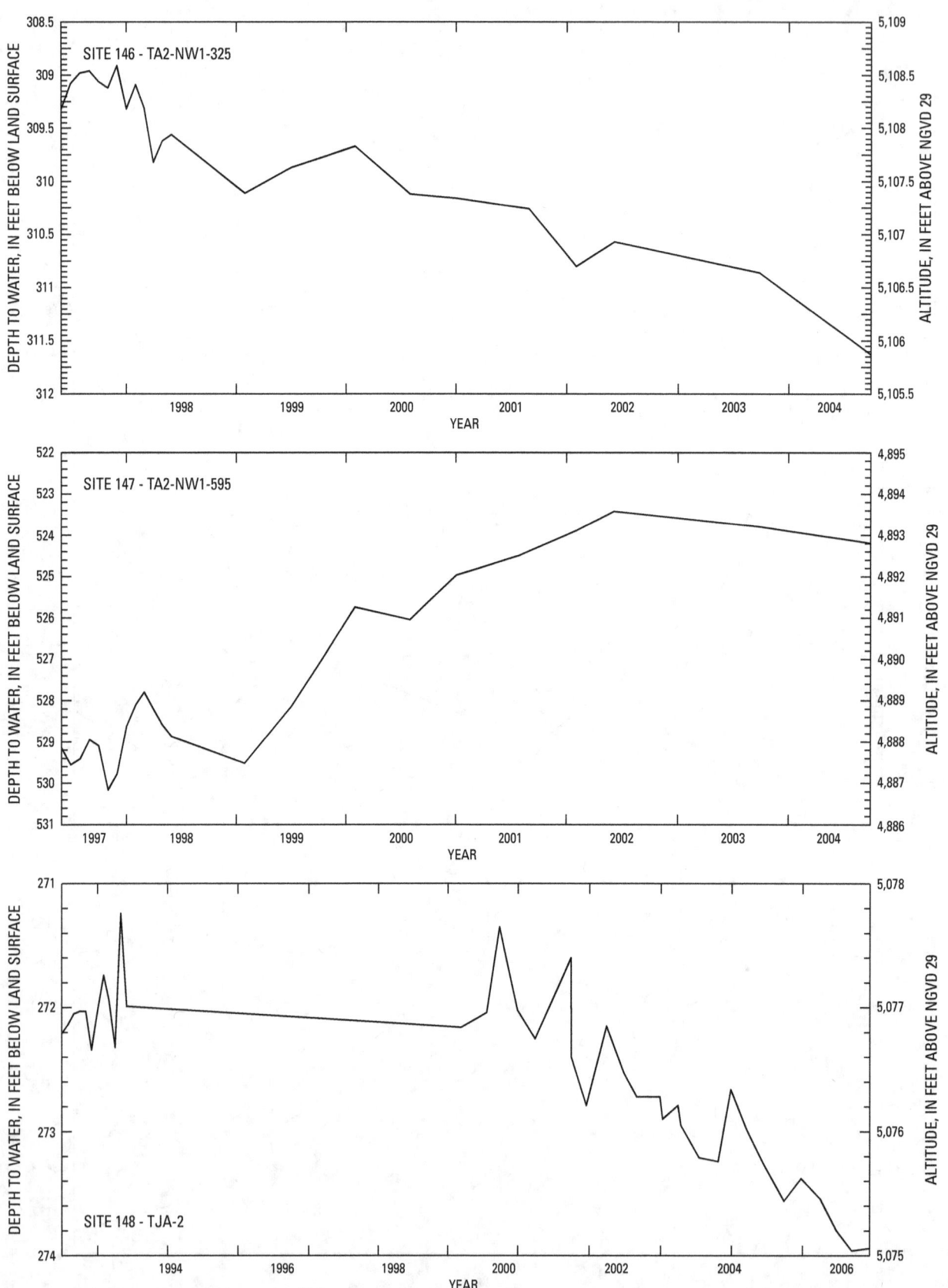

Figure 4. Water-level data for selected wells and piezometers in the Albuquerque Basin.—Continued

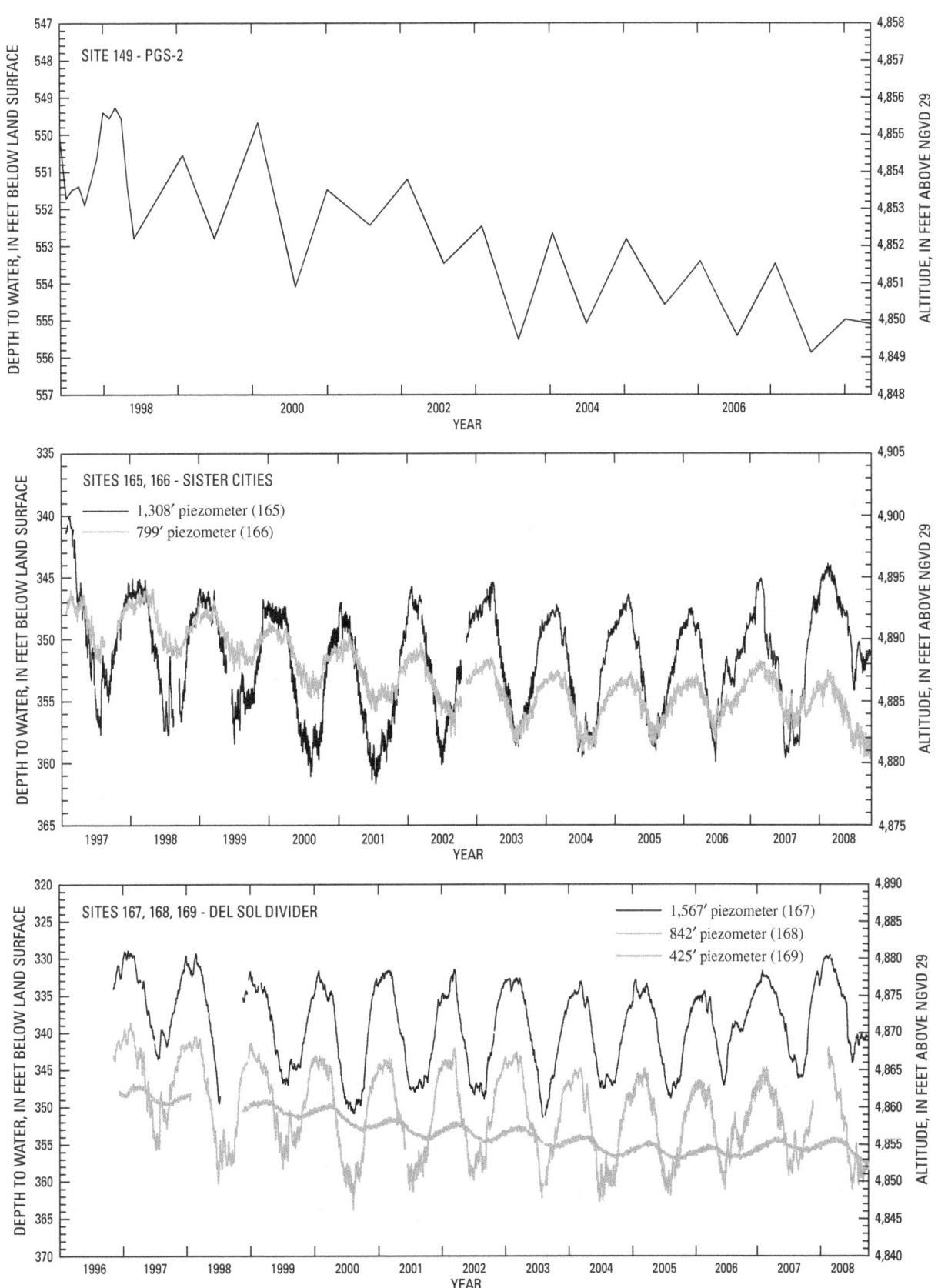

Figure 4. Water-level data for selected wells and piezometers in the Albuquerque Basin.—Continued

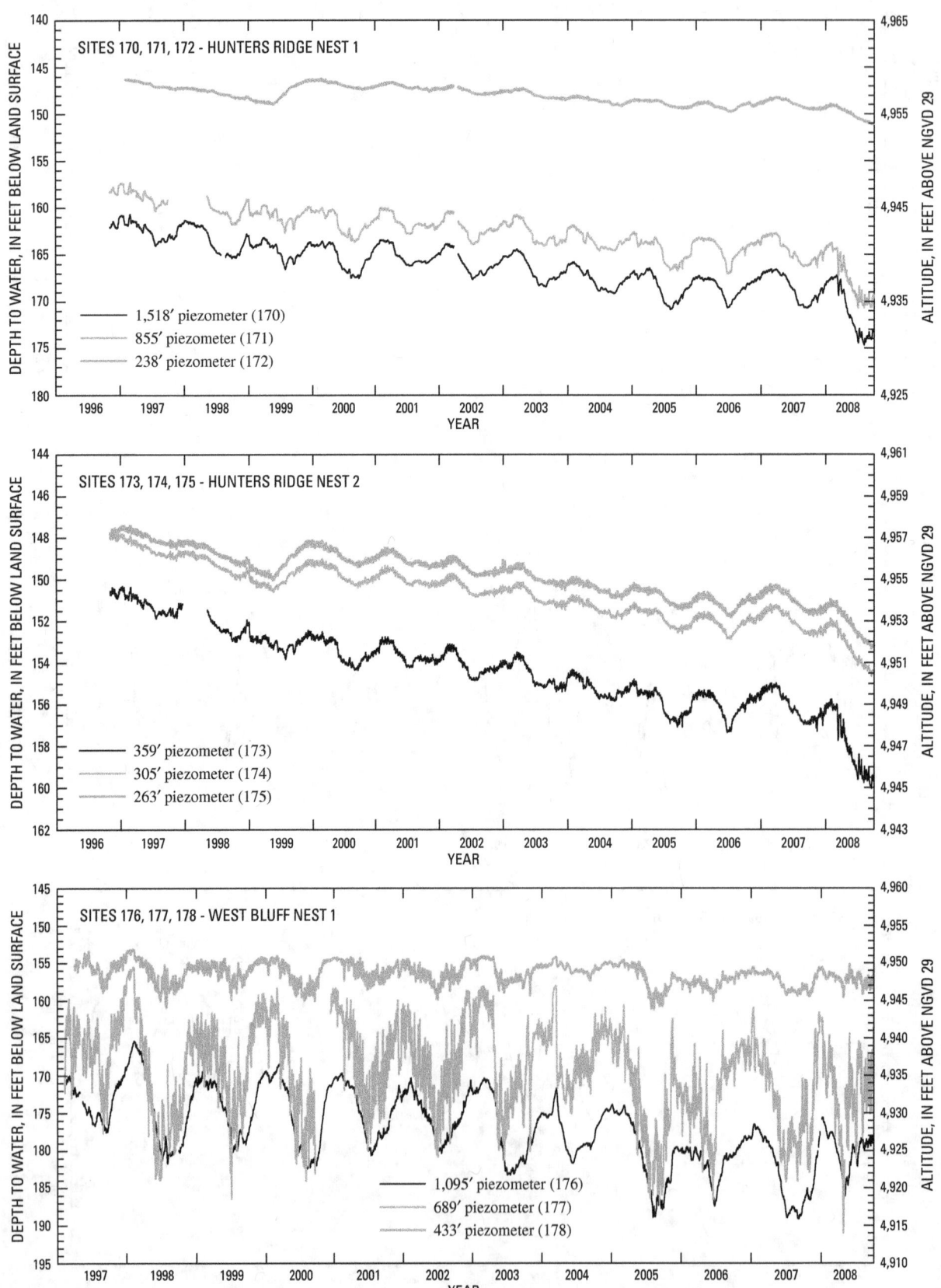

Figure 4. Water-level data for selected wells and piezometers in the Albuquerque Basin.—Continued

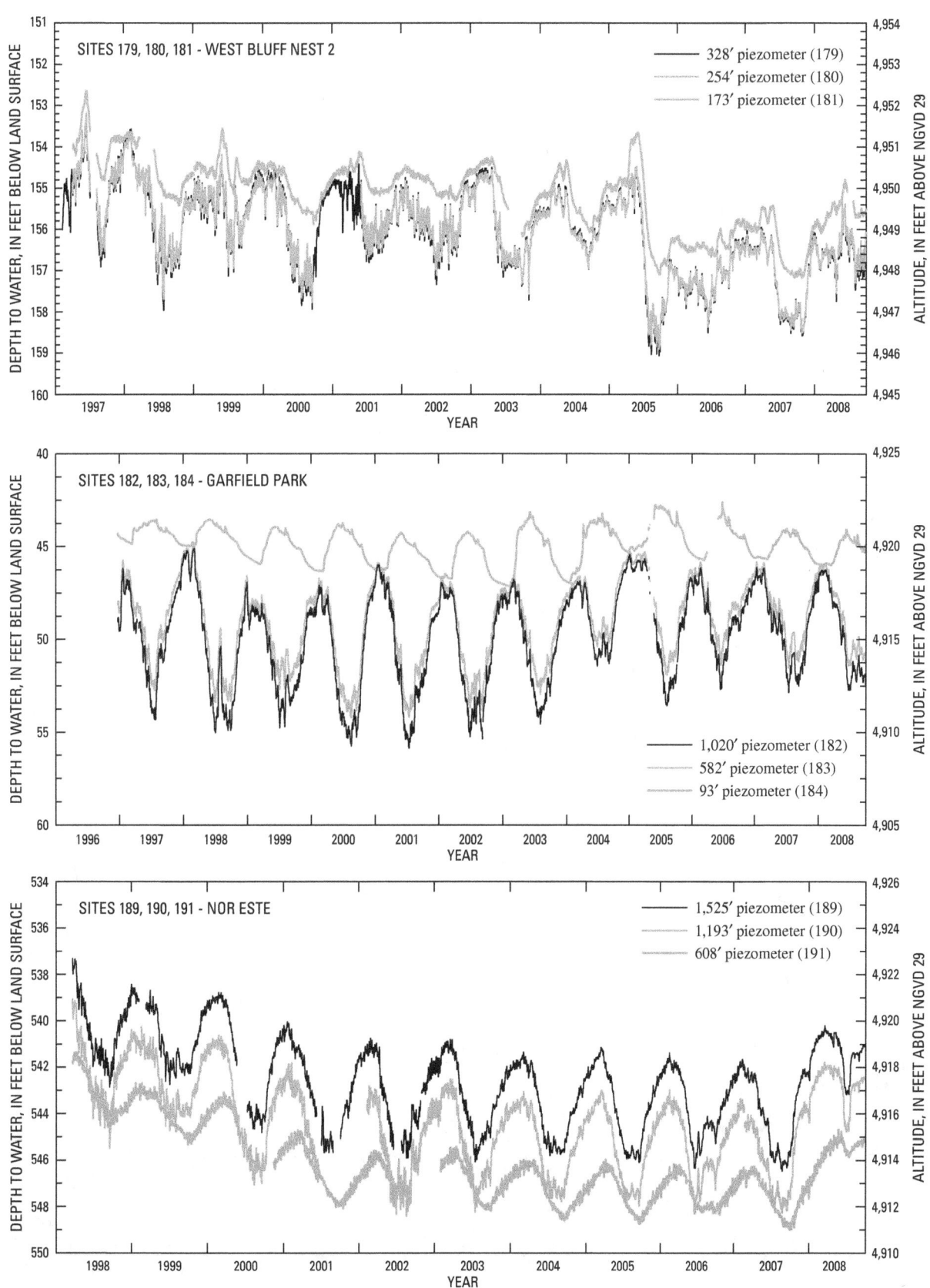

Figure 4. Water-level data for selected wells and piezometers in the Albuquerque Basin.—Continued

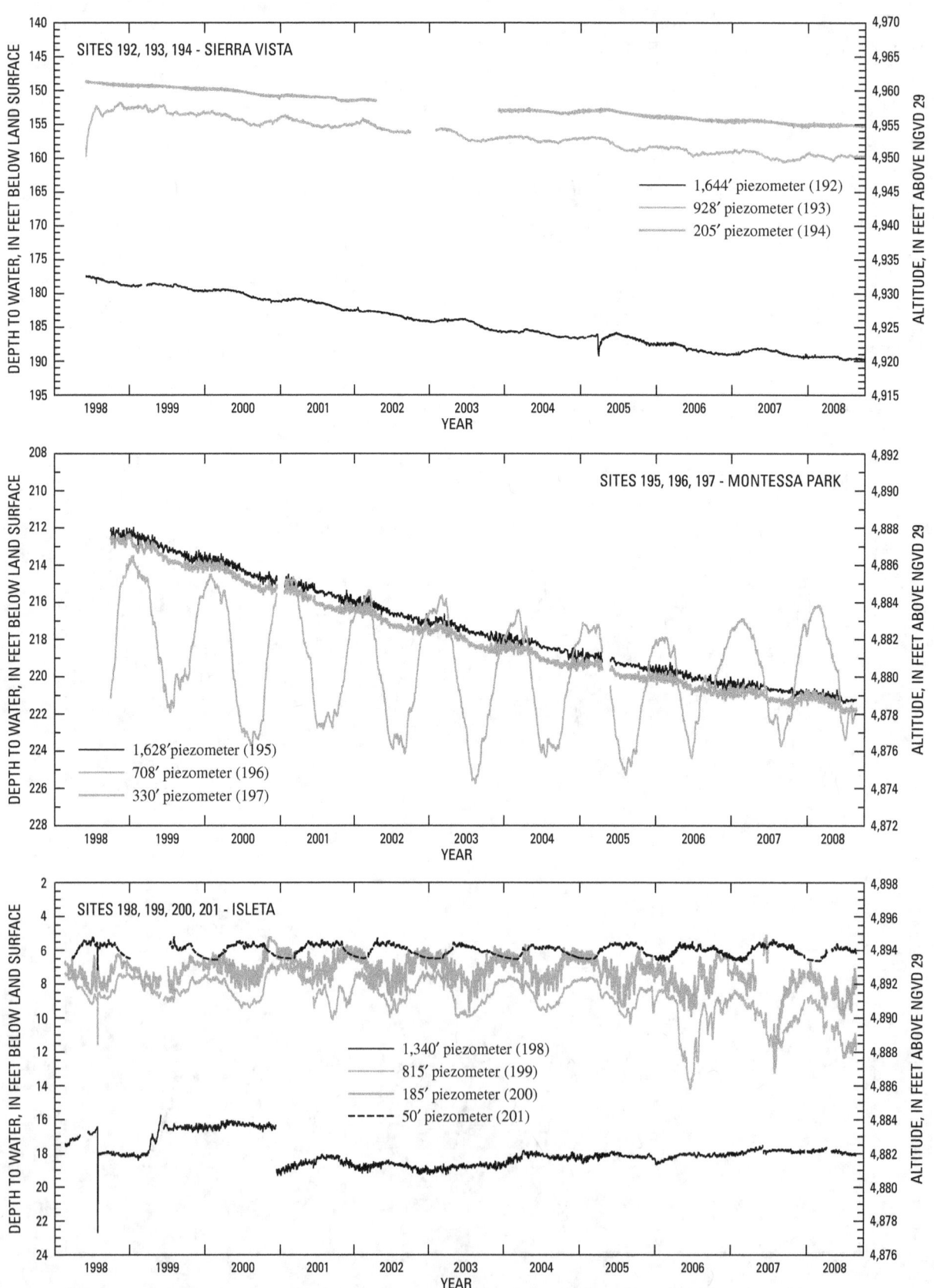

Figure 4.   Water-level data for selected wells and piezometers in the Albuquerque Basin.—Continued

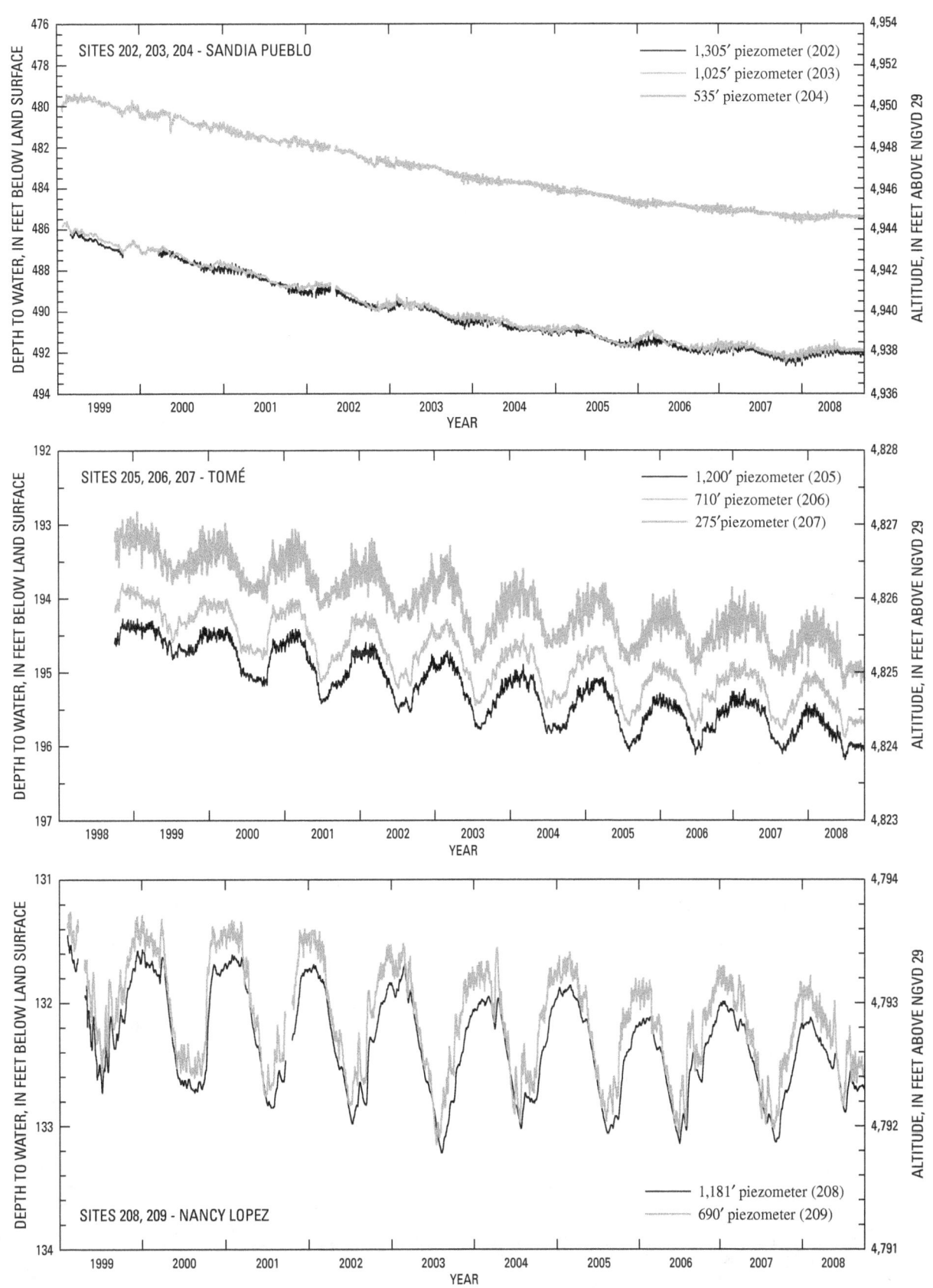

Figure 4.   Water-level data for selected wells and piezometers in the Albuquerque Basin.—Continued

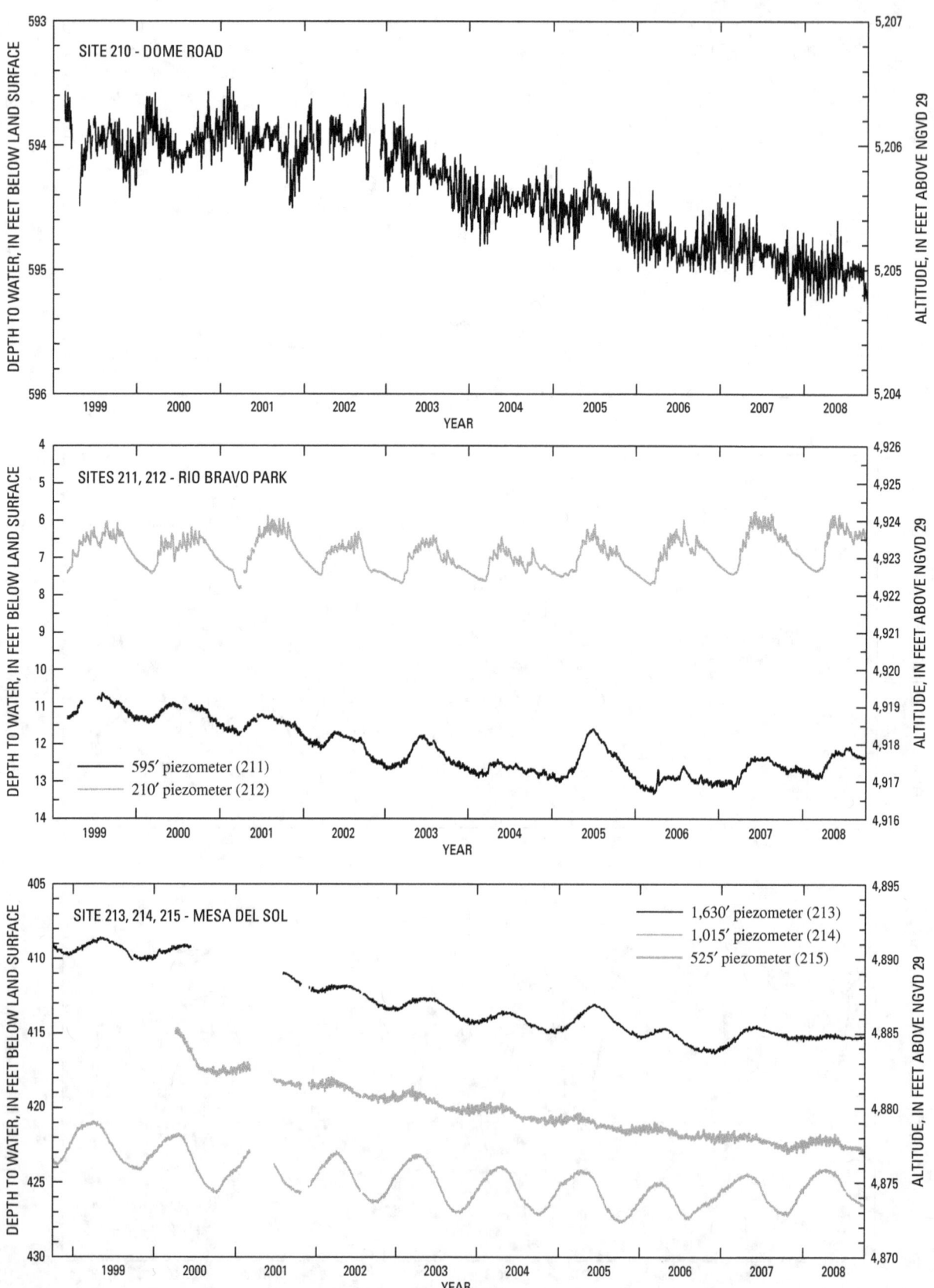

Figure 4. Water-level data for selected wells and piezometers in the Albuquerque Basin.—Continued

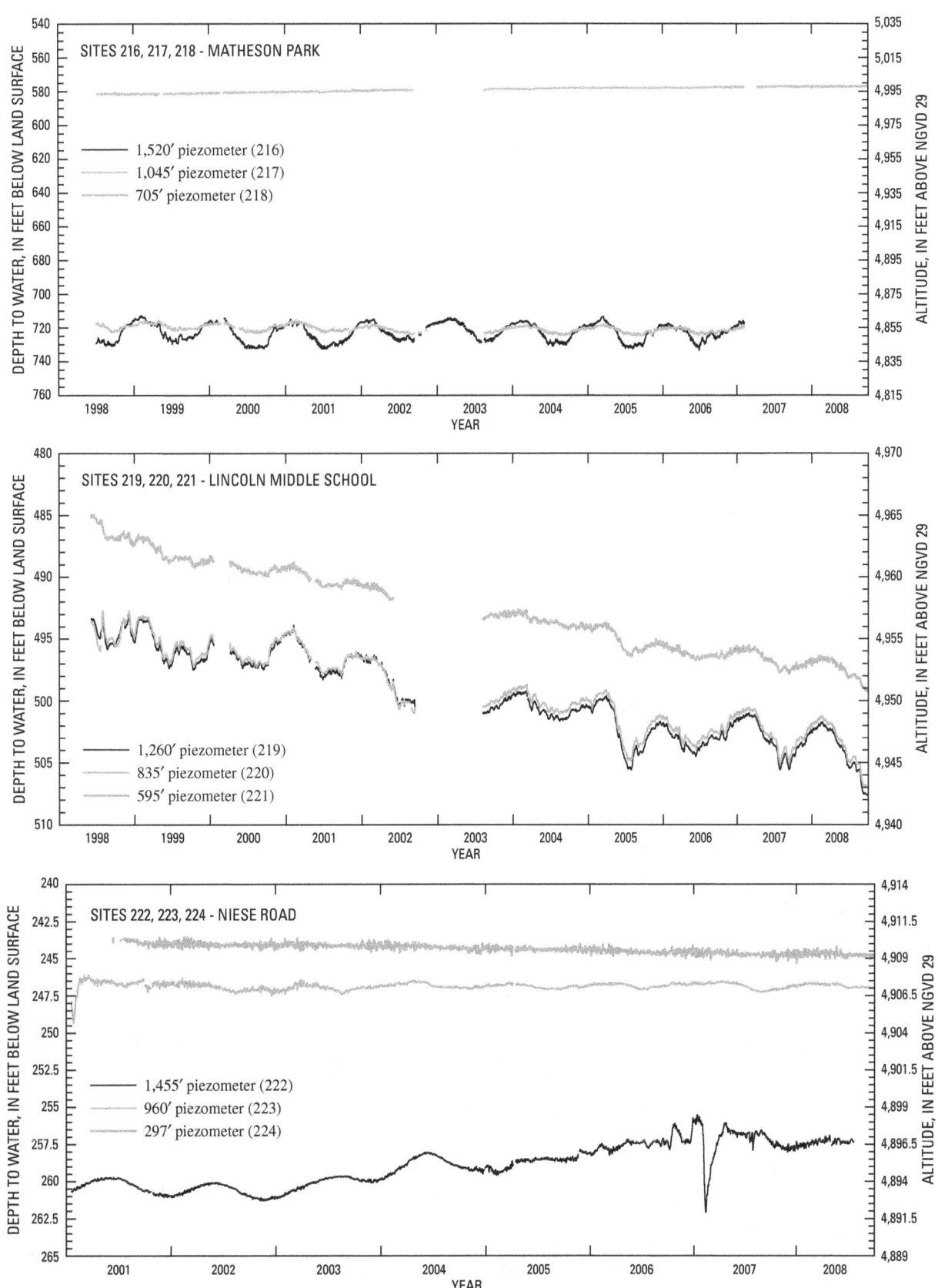

Figure 4. Water-level data for selected wells and piezometers in the Albuquerque Basin.—Continued

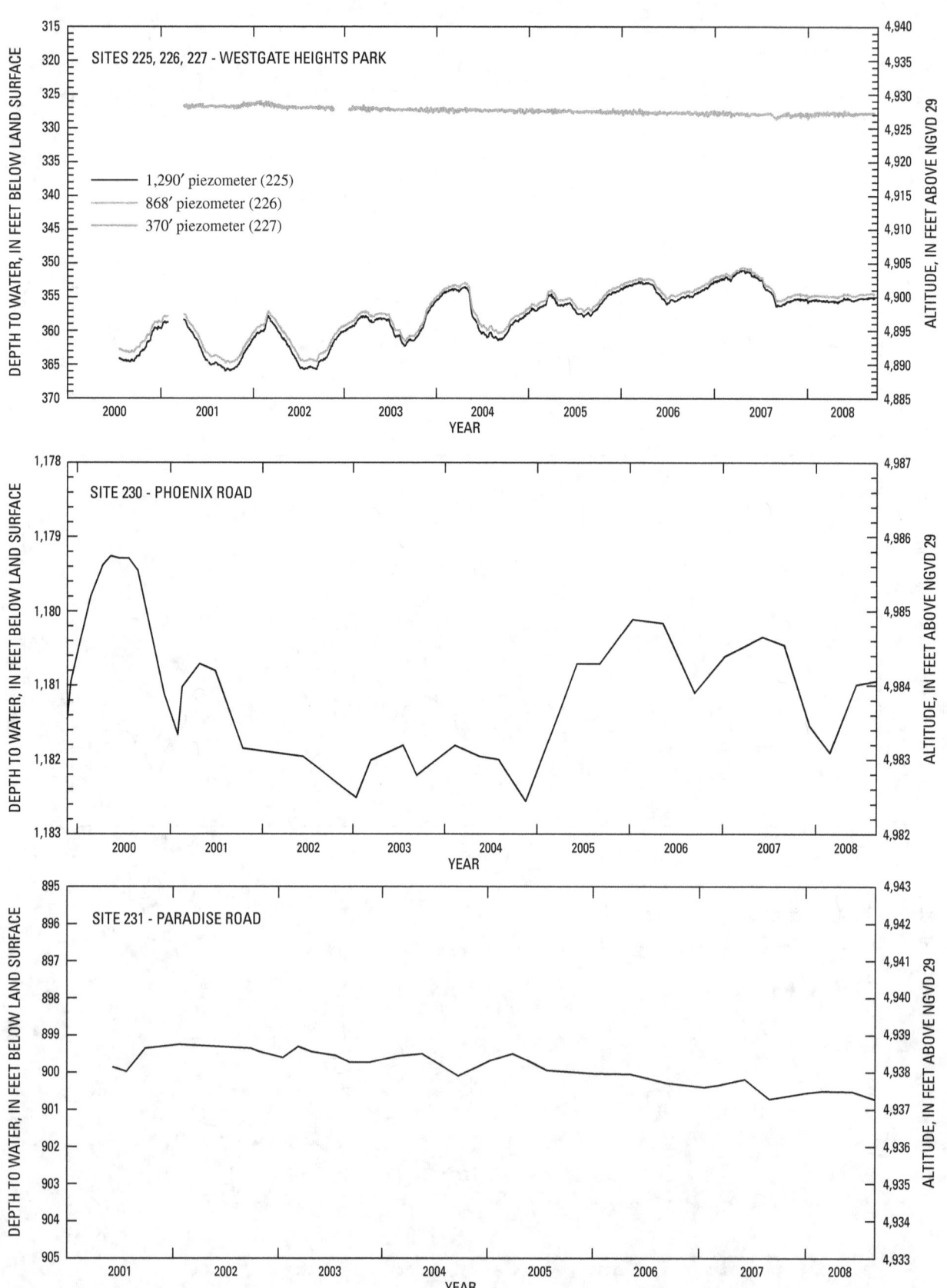

Figure 4. Water-level data for selected wells and piezometers in the Albuquerque Basin.—Continued

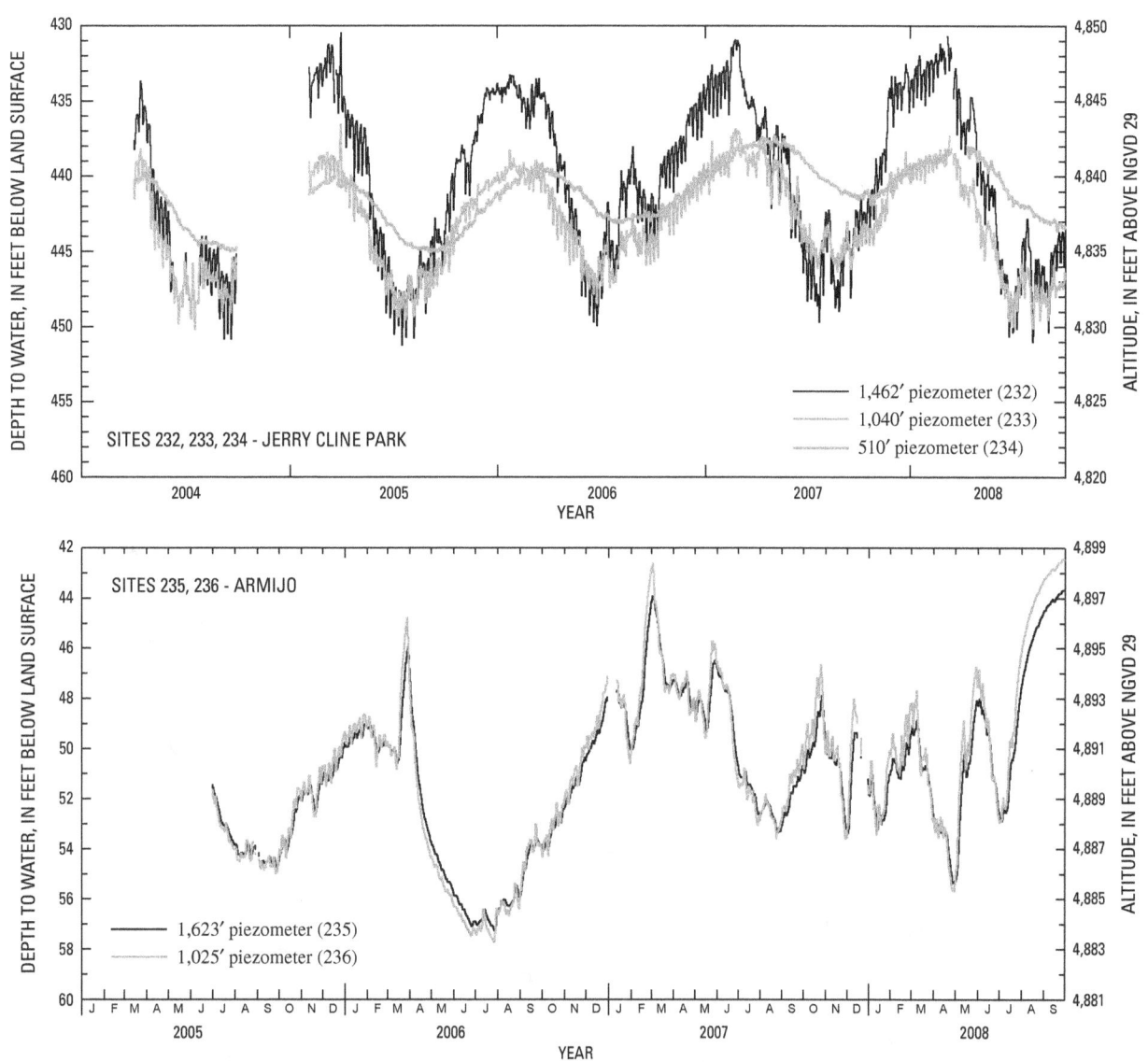

Figure 4.   Water-level data for selected wells and piezometers in the Albuquerque Basin.—Continued

Publishing support provided by:
Denver Publishing Service Center

For more information concerning this publication, contact:
Director, New Mexico Water Science Center
U.S. Geological Survey
5338 Montgomery Boulevard NE
Albuquerque, New Mexico 87109-1311
(505) 830-7900

Or visit the New Mexico Water Science Center Web site at:
http://nm.water.usgs.gov/

USGS

Beman—Water-Level Data for the Albuquerque Basin and Adjacent Areas, New Mexico, Period of Record Through September 30, 2008—Open-File Report 2009-1125

ISBN 978-1-4113-2923-2

9 781411 329232

 Printed on recycled paper